Microwave Magic
Sauces and Soups

Grolier Limited
TORONTO

Contributors to this series:

Recipes and Technical Assistance:
École de cuisine Bachand-Bissonnette
Cooking consultants:
Denis Bissonette
Michèle Émond
Dietician:
Christiane Barbeau
Photos:
Laramée Morel Communications
Audio-Visuelles
Design:
Claudette Taillefer
Assistants:
Julie Deslauriers
Philippe O'Connor
Joan Pothier
Accessories:
Andrée Cournoyer
Writing:
Communications La Griffe Inc.
Text Consultants:
Cap et bc inc.
Advisors:
Roger Aubin
Joseph R. De Varennes
Gaston Lavoie
Kenneth H. Pearson

Assembly:
Carole Garon
Vital Lapalme
Jean-Pierre Larose
Carl Simmons
Gus Soriano
Marc Vallières
Production Managers:
Gilles Chamberland
Ernest Homewood
Production Assistants:
Martine Gingras
Catherine Gordon
Kathy Kishimoto
Peter Thomlison
Art Director:
Bernard Lamy
Editors:
Laurielle Ilacqua
Susan Marshall
Margaret Oliver
Robin Rivers
Lois Rock
Jocelyn Smyth
Donna Thomson
Dolores Williams
Development:
Le Groupe Polygone Éditeurs Inc.

We wish to thank the following firms, PIER I IMPORTS and LE CACHE POT, for their contribution to the illustration of this set.

The series editors have taken every care to ensure that the information given is accurate. However, no cookbook can guarantee the user successful results. The editors cannot accept any responsibility for the results obtained by following the recipes and recommendations given.

Canadian Cataloguing in Publication Data

Main entry under title:

Sauces and soups

(Microwave magic ; 11)
Translation of: Sauces et potages.
Includes index.
ISBN 0-7172-2432-5

1. Sauces.   2. Soups.   I. Series: Microwave magic
(Toronto, Ont.) ; 11.

TX832.S3813 1988   641.8'14   C88-094210-X

Contents

Microwave Magic is a multi-volume set, with each volume devoted to a particular type of cooking. So, if you are looking for a chicken recipe, you simply go to one of the two volumes that deal with poultry. Each volume has its own index, and the final volume contains a general index to the complete set.

Microwave Magic puts over twelve hundred recipes at your fingertips. You will find it as useful as the microwave oven itself. Enjoy!

Note from the Editor

How to Use this Book
The books in this set have been designed to make your job as easy as possible. As a result, most of the recipes are set out in a standard way.

We suggest that you begin by consulting the information chart for the recipe you have chosen. You will find there all the information you need to decide if you are able to make it: preparation time, cost per serving, level of difficulty, number of calories per serving and other relevant details. Thus, if you have only 30 minutes in which to prepare the evening meal, you will quickly be able to tell which recipe is possible and suits your schedule.

The list of ingredients is always clearly separated from the main text. When space allows, the ingredients are shown together in a photograph so that you can make sure you have them all without rereading the list—

another way of saving your valuable time. In addition, for the more complex recipes we have supplied photographs of the key stages involved either in preparation or serving.

All the dishes in this book have been cooked in a 700 watt microwave oven. If your oven has a different wattage, consult the conversion chart that appears on the following page for cooking times in different types of oven. We would like to emphasize that the cooking times given in the book are a minimum. If a dish does not seem to be cooked enough, you may return it to the oven for a few more minutes. Also, the cooking time can vary according to your ingredients: their water and fat content, thickness, shape and even where they come from. We have therefore left a blank space on each recipe page in which you can note

the cooking time that suits you best. This will enable you to add a personal touch to the recipes that we suggest and to reproduce your best results every time.

Although we have put all the technical information together at the front of this book, we have inserted a number of boxed entries called **MICROTIPS** throughout to explain particular techniques. They are brief and simple, and will help you obtain successful results in your cooking.

With the very first recipe you try, you will discover just how simple microwave cooking can be and how often it depends on techniques you already use for cooking with a conventional oven. If cooking is a pleasure for you, as it is for us, it will be all the more so with a microwave oven. Now let's get on with the food.

The Editor

Key to the Symbols
For ease of reference, the following symbols have been used on the recipe information charts.

The pencil symbol  is a reminder to write your cooking time in the space provided.

Level of Difficulty

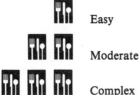

Easy

Moderate

Complex

Cost per Serving

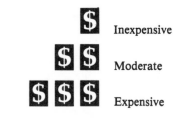

Inexpensive

Moderate

Expensive

6

Power Levels

All the recipes in this book have been tested in a 700 watt oven. As there are many microwave ovens on the market with different power levels, and as the names of these levels vary from one manufacturer to another, we have decided to give power levels as a percentage. To adapt the power levels given here, consult the chart opposite and the instruction manual for your oven.

Generally speaking, if you have a 500 watt or 600 watt oven you should increase cooking times by about 30% over those given, depending on the actual length of time required. The shorter the original cooking time, the greater the percentage by which it must be lengthened. The 30% figure is only an average. Consult the chart for detailed information on this topic.

Power Levels

HIGH: 100% - 90%	Vegetables (except boiled potatoes and carrots) Soup Sauce Fruits Browning ground beef Browning dish Popcorn
MEDIUM HIGH: 80% - 70%	Rapid defrosting of precooked dishes Muffins Some cakes Hot dogs
MEDIUM: 60% - 50%	Cooking tender meat Cakes Fish Seafood Eggs Reheating Boiled potatoes and carrots
MEDIUM LOW: 40%	Cooking less tender meat Simmering Melting chocolate
DEFROST: 30% **LOW: 30% - 20%**	Defrosting Simmering Cooking less tender meat
WARM: 10%	Keeping food warm Allowing yeast dough to rise

Cooking Time Conversion Chart

700 watts	600 watts*
5 s	11 s
15 s	20 s
30 s	40 s
45 s	1 min
1 min	1 min 20 s
2 min	2 min 40 s
3 min	4 min
4 min	5 min 20 s
5 min	6 min 40 s
6 min	8 min
7 min	9 min 20 s
8 min	10 min 40 s
9 min	12 min
10 min	13 min 30 s
20 min	26 min 40 s
30 min	40 min
40 min	53 min 40 s
50 min	66 min 40 s
1 h	1 h 20 min

* There is very little difference in cooking times between 500 watt ovens and 600 watt ovens.

Perfect Partners for a Great Meal

Do you remember ever being admonished for dipping your bread in your soup when you were a child? If so, it is not altogether surprising; in modern Western society this practice is not regarded as "proper." How times have changed! In Medieval Europe soup and bread went hand in hand as a meal in themselves. People would put a thick slice of bread in a bowl and then ladle over it generous helpings of the wonderfully thick and hearty soups that were served in those days.

Many of today's soups, however, are lighter and more refined—frequently served as appetizers prior to the main course. But whether the result is clear, creamy or heavy, the method of preparing soup is still basically the same as that of our ancestors. A variety of ingredients, in varying quantities and combinations, are added to stock and the bread is now served separately, on the side. Sauces, as pleasing as they are, are not considered essential to a meal. More optional than soups, they are "added touches," adornments to meat and vegetables. As with soups, recipes for sauces have evolved over the years to keep up with changing fashions. In the Middle Ages sauces were regarded as rustic fare and were highly seasoned. They were even frequently used to disguise food that was suspect, that had begun to go "off." The sophisticated society of seventeenth-century France, however, initiated the development of more refined sauces, known today as béchamel, velouté and espagnole—the basic white, blond and brown sauces which constitute the foundations of hundreds of others. Mayonnaise and hollandaise, sauces based on the use of eggs, belong to another category on which there are a number of variations.

Successful sauces require rather more care in their preparation than do soups. And, although regarded as added features, there is no doubt that a poorly made sauce can ruin a meal. It is therefore very important to master the basic techniques for making them.

Lovely delicate soups, stunning in their role as starters, and rich creamy sauces, dressing up the main course, both make perfect partners to any meal. The recipes offered throughout this volume will alleviate any doubt you may have as to the validity of this statement.

The Wonderful World of Sauces

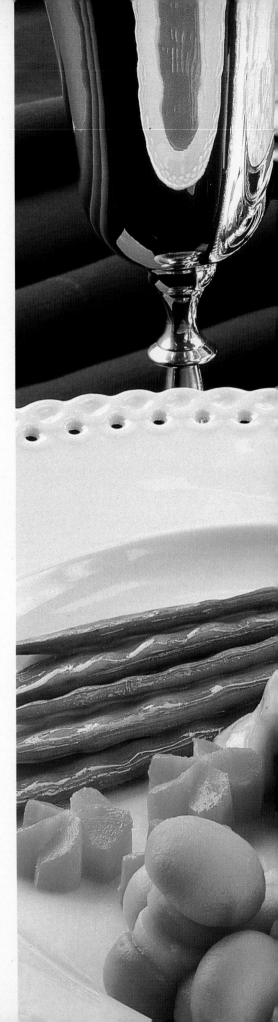

The types of sauces that are popular today were developed in seventeenth- and eighteenth-century France. Since that time, fashions have come and gone, each bringing subtle modifications to the basic techniques. In recent years, a trend known as *nouvelle cuisine* has been the rage. In this style of cooking the use of flour as a thickener is rejected; sauces are reduced to the proper consistency by boiling the liquid and allowing it to evaporate or by adding other thickening agents, such as cream, egg yolks or puréed vegetables.

There is, however, no need to be a slave to fashion. As you will discover in this volume, the techniques for making sauces are generally quite similar. Once the basic techniques have been learned, your imagination may well take over and you should be able to devise your own sauce recipes.

The range of basic ingredients used in the preparation of sauces is fairly narrow: cooking juices, stock, butter, wine, vinegar, lemon juice, milk and cream.

These ingredients are enhanced by the addition of aromatic herbs (basil, chervil, tarragon, bay leaves, marjoram, parsley, rosemary, savory and so on) or spices (cloves, nutmeg, pepper, allspice and saffron). As for thickening techniques, some sauces are based on roux (equal quantities of butter and flour, cooked to the desired color) as a thickening agent and others rely on carefully blending cream and egg yolks with a simmering liquid (such as meat, poultry or fish stock) to thicken it. Still other, more simple, sauces are brought to the proper consistency merely by combining different ingredients in certain ways. In this category we find flavored butters; vegetable purées to make such sauces as tomato sauce; vinaigrette, which combines oil with vinegar or lemon juice; and pesto, a thin paste made from garlic, oil, basil and cheese.

The microwave oven makes it easy to prepare sauces in no time at all, thereby transforming simple fare into wonderful feasts.

Hollandaise Sauce

Ingredients
6 egg yolks
200 g (7 ounces) butter
15 mL (1 tablespoon) white wine vinegar
45 mL (3 tablespoons) lemon juice
5 mL (1 teaspoon) sugar
salt and pepper to taste

Method
— Pour 500 mL (2 cups) of water into a large dish, cover and bring to the boil by cooking at 100% for 6 minutes.
— In the meantime, put the egg yolks into a bowl and whisk.
— Remove the dish of boiling water from the oven and place the bowl containing the egg yolks in the center.
— Set the power level at 30% and heat the bowl of egg yolks standing in the boiling water for 3 minutes, whisking well every minute. Set aside.
— Heat the butter at 100% for 1-1/2 minutes; remove from the oven and skim the foam from the surface.
— Add the melted butter, little by little, to the egg yolks, whisking vigorously all the while.
— Combine the vinegar and lemon juice in a small bowl and heat at 30% for 30 seconds; pour in a thin stream into the egg yolks, whisking constantly.
— Add the sugar, salt and pepper and mix well.
— If a thicker consistency is desired, reheat the sauce at 30% for 2 minutes, whisking after one minute. Do not allow the sauce to boil.

Béchamel Sauce

This wonderful creamy sauce, the mother
of all white sauces, goes very well with an
infinite number of dishes.

The proportions listed below yield a sauce
of medium thickness. To obtain a thinner
sauce, use only 45 mL (3 tablespoons)
butter and 45 mL (3 tablespoons) flour; if
you want a thicker sauce, allow 75 mL
(5 tablespoons) butter and 75 mL
(5 tablespoons) flour.

Ingredients
60 mL (4 tablespoons) butter
60 mL (4 tablespoons) flour
500 mL (2 cups) milk
salt and pepper to taste

Method
— Put the butter in a dish and heat at
  100% for 1-1/2 minutes.
— Add the flour and mix well.
— Blend in the milk, beating with a whisk,
  and season.
— Cook at 100% for 5 to 7 minutes,
  whisking every 2 minutes.

MICROTIPS

Deglazing

To deglaze a pan, simply add a little liquid to it and whisk vigorously to incorporate the cooking juices and to lift all the flavorful food particles. A wide range of liquids may be used, depending on the dish you are making. Your options include wine, spirits, beer, cider, vinegar, cream, stock, vegetable or fruit juice and even water. Remember that wine loses its acid taste when it is cooked.

Next, allow the liquid to simmer until it is reduced to the proper consistency. It can be served as it is or blended with other ingredients, such as clear or thickened stock or a vegetable purée, depending on the dish it is to accompany. Flavoring agents such as chopped green onions and garlic may also be added. Note that you should add fresh herbs at the last minute so that their distinctive flavor is not destroyed by overcooking.

If further thickening is required, consult "Microtips" on page 15, opposite, for different options in terms of thickening agents.

Mornay Sauce

This is a variation on béchamel sauce that goes particularly well with fish and vegetable dishes as well as with poached eggs.

Ingredients
250 mL (1 cup) béchamel sauce of medium thickness (see basic recipe, page 13)
2 egg yolks
125 mL (1/2 cup) 18% cream
125 mL (1/2 cup) cheese of your choice, grated

Method
— Heat the béchamel sauce at 100% for 2 to 3 minutes, beating with a whisk every minute.
— Combine the egg yolks and cream in a bowl and mix well.
— Add a little of the heated béchamel to the egg and cream mixture and then slowly add this mixture to the béchamel, whisking constantly.
— Add the cheese, beating constantly.
— Heat at 100% for 1 to 2 minutes, whisking after 40 seconds, but do not allow the sauce to boil.

MICROTIPS

Thickening Agents

Food products containing a large quantity of starch, such as flour, cornstarch and arrowroot are commonly used to thicken sauces. In using these products, however, you must cook the sauce long enough to eliminate any floury taste.

Beurre manié is made with a mixture of equal quantities of uncooked butter and flour that are kneaded together. It is added, little by little, to boiling sauce or stock and it is vital that you beat your mixture constantly to ensure that the end product is smooth and free from lumps.

A mixture of egg yolks and cream, known as a *liaison,* adds richness as well as thickening properties to sauces. It is a good idea to incorporate a little of the hot liquid into these ingredients *before* adding to the entire quantity to avoid curdling. You should also make sure that the sauce does not come to the boil once these ingredients have been added.

Another excellent thickening agent is roux, equal quantities of cooked butter and flour, to which the liquid to be thickened is added.

Béarnaise Sauce

An ideal sauce to serve with steak, some green vegetables and fish.

Ingredients

4 egg yolks
10 mL (2 teaspoons) white vinegar
5 mL (1 teaspoon) onion flakes
5 mL (1 teaspoon) tarragon
2 mL (1/2 teaspoon) chervil
white pepper to taste
125 mL (1/2 cup) butter
5 mL (1 teaspoon) fresh parsley

Method

— Put the egg yolks, vinegar, onion flakes and spices in a blender.
— Heat the butter at 100% for 1 to 2 minutes.
— Blend the ingredients at high speed and gradually add the melted butter until the sauce is thick and creamy.
— Pour the resulting sauce into a serving bowl; sprinkle with parsley and serve immediately.

Sauces for Seafood

Fish and seafood are finally gaining some long-deserved popularity in North America. Some varieties are economical and all are highly nutritious, rich in vitamins and minerals but low in fat. They are quicker and easier to prepare than many meats or poultry and can be served in a number of different ways. Fish and seafood may be poached, steamed, braised, stewed, baked or broiled. They may also be eaten raw, in the Japanese tradition, cut into thin slices or slivers and marinated in lime or lemon juice, soy sauce, mustard and horseradish.

There are many types of sauces that go well with fish and seafood, as you will discover in the following pages. However, as with sauces for meat and poultry, an awareness of what sauces are suitable for serving with what type of seafood is well worth having. Once a few basic guidelines are understood, you can start developing your own recipes.

A traditional béchamel sauce, which is smooth and delicately flavored, goes well with many types of fish. If you add lemon juice and aromatic herbs, such as coriander and mint, you have Lemon Sauce, which is just perfect with microwaved fillets of sole. Parmesan Sauce, made with cream, stock and Parmesan cheese, is somewhat richer. You can also add a pinch of nutmeg and a knob of butter and serve it with fish that has been poached in a rich fish stock. Other frequent combinations include Hollandaise with poached fish, Sweet and Sour Sauce with shrimp, Cucumber and Dill Sauce with cold poached salmon and Watercress Sauce with sole.

Many sauces that go well with fish and seafood are made with roux as their thickening agent. Provençale Sauce, which gets its distinctive color and flavor from a combination of tomatoes and aromatic herbs, goes especially well with fish that has been coated in flour and baked. Espagnole Sauce, thicker and having a stronger flavor, is best with poached fish.

The slightly acid taste of mayonnaise forms the basis of many cold sauces. One classic example is Tartar Sauce which can be served with fish and seafood alike. (Note, however, that on page 18 we offer a less traditional recipe for Tartar Sauce, one that is served hot.) Herring, sardines and broiled mackerel are excellent served cold with a sauce made with mayonnaise and a little mustard.

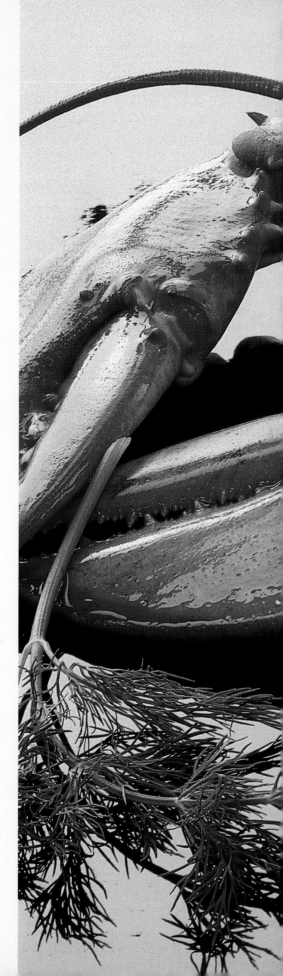

Sweet and Sour Sauce

Ingredients
30 mL (2 tablespoons) sugar
15 mL (1 tablespoon) cornstarch
2 mL (1/2 teaspoon) chili powder
150 mL (2/3 cup) water
45 mL (3 tablespoons) ketchup
15 mL (1 tablespoon) cider vinegar
50 mL (1/4 cup) relish or sweet pickles, chopped

Method
— Combine all the ingredients except the relish or pickles in a bowl and mix well until they are smoothly blended.
— Cook at 100% for 10 to 11 minutes or until the mixture thickens, stirring twice.
— Add the relish or pickles and heat at 50% for 1 minute. Serve hot or cold.

Tartar Sauce

The following recipe for tartar sauce, normally a variation on mayonnaise and served cold, has an incomparable flavor when it is served hot.

Ingredients
22 mL (1-1/2 tablespoons) butter
22 mL (1-1/2 tablespoons) flour
250 mL (1 cup) milk
15 mL (1 tablespoon) lemon juice
7 mL (1-1/2 teaspoons) capers, finely chopped
60 mL (4 tablespoons) relish or sweet pickles, chopped
1 egg yolk
250 mL (1 cup) 35% cream

Method
— Put the butter in a dish and heat at 100% for 30 seconds. Add the flour and mix well.
— Add the milk and cook at 100% for 3 to 4 minutes, stirring every minute.
— Add the lemon juice, capers and relish or pickles and mix well.
— Combine the egg yolk with the cream in a bowl and whisk well; add this mixture to the hot milk mixture and mix well.
— Reduce the power level to 70% and heat for 1 to 2 minutes, but do not allow the sauce to boil.

Butter and Dill Sauce

Ingredients
250 mL (1 cup) butter
10 mL (2 teaspoons) dried dill
1 mL (1/4 teaspoon) salt

Method
— Put the butter in a dish and heat at 100% for 2 minutes.
— Add the dill and salt; mix well and serve immediately.

Cucumber and Dill Sauce

Ingredients
1 cucumber, peeled, seeded and chopped
250 mL (8 oz) sour cream
5 mL (1 teaspoon) dried dill
5 mL (1 teaspoon) sugar
salt and pepper to taste

Method
— Combine all the ingredients in a bowl and mix well.
— Chill for 1 hour before serving.

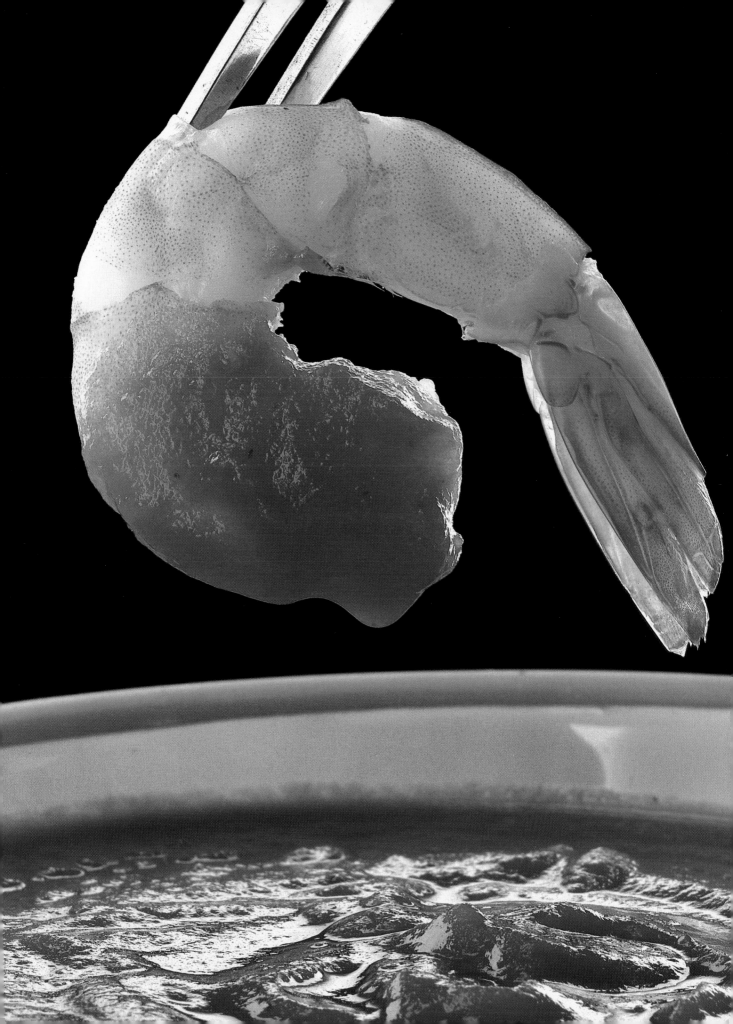

Watercress Sauce

Ingredients
1 bunch watercress, chopped
1 onion, finely chopped
1 clove garlic, cut into two
75 mL (1/3 cup) butter
50 mL (1/4 cup) white wine

Method
— Combine the onion, garlic and butter and cook at 100% for 3 to 4 minutes, stirring once.
— Remove the garlic and add the white wine and the watercress.
— Cover and cook at 100% for 2 to 3 minutes or until the watercress is tender, stirring once during the cooking time.

Lemon Sauce

Ingredients
juice of 1 lemon
zest of 1 lemon
30 mL (2 tablespoons) butter
30 mL (2 tablespoons) flour
250 mL (1 cup) milk
coriander to taste
crushed mint to taste
salt and pepper to taste

Method
— Put the butter in a dish and heat at 100% for 40 seconds.
— Add the flour and mix well.
— Add the milk, beating with a wire whisk.
— Cook at 100% for 3 to 4 minutes, whisking after 2 minutes.
— Add the lemon juice, lemon zest, coriander and mint.
— Season to taste and serve.

MICROTIPS

To Cook Fish Successfully

Fish is done when the flesh comes away from the backbone easily and is tender, opaque and milky. Overcooked fish is firm and solid rather than light and flaky. It is worth testing for doneness a little before the end of the recommended cooking time as individual fish require slightly different cooking times, depending on such factors as their thickness and water content.

Never add salt to the fish before the end of the cooking time unless the recipe specifically tells you to do so; salt extracts the juices from the flesh, which results in loss of flavor and texture.

Poaching is best suited to fish with firm flesh, such as salmon, turbot and sole. It also works well with shellfish. However, do not use this method with fish that have delicate flesh as they tend to disintegrate.

Fish or seafood may be poached in water, but using a court bouillon or a concentrated fish stock known as a fumet will greatly enhance the flavor. Court bouillon is made with water, vegetables, aromatic seasonings, and an acidic liquid such as lemon juice, cider, vinegar or wine. Be cautious when adding wine to a court bouillon—too much can easily overpower the flavor of some types of fish. If you add fish trimmings to the cooking liquid you will have a fumet which can be used to make sauces and soups. Milk is sometimes used in court bouillon as well, imparting a milder flavor and keeping the fish fillets beautifully white as they cook.

If you plan to broil fish, use vegetable oil. It doesn't burn and has a less pronounced flavor than other types of cooking oil.

Parmesan Sauce

Ingredients
125 mL (1/2 cup) Parmesan cheese, grated
50 mL (1/4 cup) butter
50 mL (1/4 cup) flour
375 mL (1-1/2 cups) 10% cream
375 mL (1-1/2 cups) chicken stock
salt and pepper to taste

Method
— Put the butter in a dish and heat at
  100% for 1 minute.
— Add the flour and mix well.
— Add the cream and chicken stock and
  cook at 100% for 6 to 8 minutes or
  until the mixture thickens, whisking
  every 2 minutes.
— Add the grated Parmesan and beat until
  it melts in the hot sauce mixture.
— Season to taste before serving.

Mustard Sauce

Ingredients
15 mL (1 tablespoon) Dijon mustard
125 mL (1/2 cup) mayonnaise
45 mL (3 tablespoons) milk
pinch salt

Method
— Combine all the ingredients in a bowl
  and mix well.
— Chill for 2 hours before serving.

Espagnole Sauce

Ingredients
60 g (2 oz) butter
2 carrots, grated
1 onion, finely chopped
60 g (2 oz) mushrooms, chopped
2 slices bacon, diced
2 sticks celery, finely chopped
60 g (2 oz) flour
500 mL (2 cups) beef stock
15 mL (1 tablespoon) tomato paste
2 tomatoes, peeled and chopped
1 bay leaf
30 mL (2 tablespoons) parsley, chopped
salt and pepper to taste

Method
— Put the butter in a dish and heat at
  100% for 1 minute; add the carrots,
  onion, mushrooms, bacon and celery.
— Cover and cook at 100% for 2 to 3
  minutes or until the vegetables and
  bacon are done, stirring halfway
  through the cooking time.
— Add the flour and mix well.
— Add the beef stock, tomato paste,
  tomatoes, bay leaf and parsley and mix
  well.
— Cover and cook at 100% for 10
  minutes.
— Reduce the power level to 90% and
  leave to simmer for 20 minutes,
  skimming the surface several times and
  stirring the mixture twice during the
  cooking time.
— Strain through a sieve and season to
  taste.

Newburg Sauce

Ingredients
2 egg yolks
375 mL (1-1/2 cups) 18% cream
75 mL (1/3 cup) butter
45 mL (3 tablespoons) flour
30 mL (2 tablespoons) sherry
pinch nutmeg
pinch cayenne
2 mL (1/2 teaspoon) lemon juice
salt and pepper to taste

Method
— Combine the egg yolks with a little of
  the cream; mix well and set aside.
— Put the butter in a dish and heat at
  100% for 1 minute; add the flour and
  mix well.
— Add the remaining cream and beat with
  a whisk.
— Cook at 100% for 4 to 5 minutes or
  until the mixture thickens, stirring twice
  during the cooking time.
— Add the sherry, nutmeg, cayenne and
  lemon juice; add a little of the mixture
  to the egg yolks and cream and mix
  well.
— Combine the two mixtures and beat
  with a whisk.
— Heat at 100% for 1 minute, stirring
  after 40 seconds; do not allow the sauce
  to boil.

Soubise Sauce

Ingredients
1 onion, finely chopped
500 mL (2 cups) béchamel sauce (see basic
recipe, page 13)
75 mL (1/3 cup) 35% cream
2 mL (1/2 teaspoon) coriander

Method
— Put the onion in a covered dish and
  cook at 100% for 2 to 3 minutes.
— Add the cooked onion to the béchamel
  sauce and then add the cream and
  coriander.
— Mix well and heat at 100% for 1 to 2
  minutes or until the sauce is hot, but do
  not allow it to boil.

Horseradish Sauce

Ingredients
50 mL (1/4 cup) horseradish, grated
10 mL (2 teaspoons) sugar
10 mL (2 teaspoons) white vinegar
500 mL (2 cups) béchamel sauce (see basic
recipe, page 13)
125 mL (1/2 cup) 35% cream

Method
— Put the horseradish, sugar and vinegar
  in a bowl and mix well.
— Add the mixture to the béchamel sauce,
  mix well and then add the cream.
— Beat with a whisk and heat at 100% for
  2 to 3 minutes or until the mixture is
  hot, but do not allow it to boil.

Caper Sauce

Ingredients
30 mL (2 tablespoons) capers
30 mL (2 tablespoons) butter
1 onion, finely chopped
30 mL (2 tablespoons) flour
250 mL (1 cup) milk
pinch curry powder
salt and pepper

Method
— Put the butter in a dish and heat at 100% for 40 seconds.
— Add the onion and cook at 100% for 2 minutes.
— Add the flour and mix well.
— Add the milk and cook at 100% for 3 to 4 minutes or until the mixture thickens, stirring every 2 minutes.
— Add the capers and curry powder; season to taste.

Provençale Sauce

Ingredients
30 mL (2 tablespoons) butter
30 mL (2 tablespoons) flour
125 mL (1/2 cup) 18% cream
125 mL (1/2 cup) beef consommé
15 mL (1 tablespoon) olive oil
2 cloves garlic, crushed
1 onion, finely chopped
2 tomatoes, peeled and cut into small pieces
30 mL (2 tablespoons) fresh parsley, chopped

Method
— Put the butter in a dish and heat at 100% for 40 seconds.
— Add the flour and mix well.
— Add the cream and beef consommé; cook at 100% for 3 to 4 minutes or until the mixture thickens, stirring twice during the cooking time; set aside.
— In another dish, combine the oil, garlic, onion, tomatoes and parsley; cover and cook at 100% for 3 to 4 minutes, stirring once during the cooking time.
— Combine the two mixtures; reduce the power level to 70% and heat through for 2 minutes, stirring once, before serving.

Best Dressed Chicken

Chicken and other types of poultry can be served in many different ways: hot or cold; poached, boiled, broiled, roasted or braised; with sauce or in a salad. The carcass and the giblets are used to make stock for a number of soups and sauces. Chicken, capon and turkey are the most well-known types of poultry in Canada. Wild duck with orange sauce, which was a treat in pioneer days, is also quite popular.

Goose, guinea fowl, and pheasant are less common and consequently more expensive. They are generally reserved for very special occasions. Hunters can obtain partridge for themselves and their friends. It is usually cooked with cabbage or as part of a casserole dish with wine or fruit juice.

The sauce recipes on the following pages are all excellent with chicken and turkey, but you should try them with other types of poultry as well. You will find a recipe for Cranberry Sauce, an old favorite with a surprising new variation.

Notice the frequency with which roux is used to make sauces for poultry. It is the basis of Madeira Sauce, which goes best with boneless breast meat that has been delicately poached. There is a creamy Chicken Velouté Sauce to serve with chicken breasts and a rich Vaucluse Sauce based on the recipe for Hollandaise Sauce in the first section of this volume. The recipe for Béchamel Sauce with Peppers uses three types of peppers; it is extremely easy to make and is simply wonderful with roast chicken or turkey.

There are several other treats in store in the pages that follow as well as ideas to spark your own creativity. Think, for example, about your *mirepoix,* the bed of aromatic vegetables that you braise with birds such as chicken and capon to enhance their delicate flavor. These vegetables can be puréed and added to a sauce or to the cooking liquid, thickened with cream and/or egg yolk. Add a dash of wine for extra flavor. The resulting sauce can be served with the poultry itself or used in some other way. Experiment with aromatics and spices when cooking poultry as well as with the sauces to accompany it. Clever combinations will enable you to turn ordinary food into a gourmet treat.

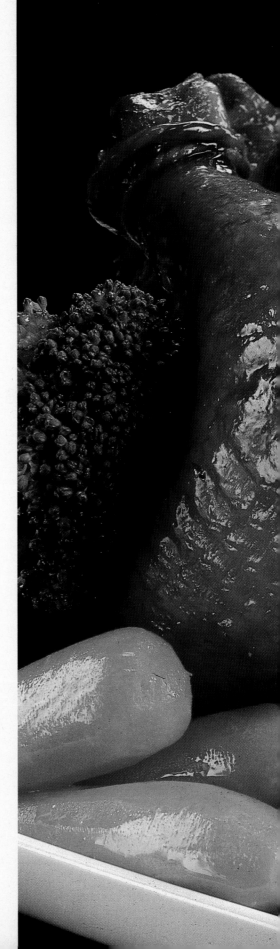

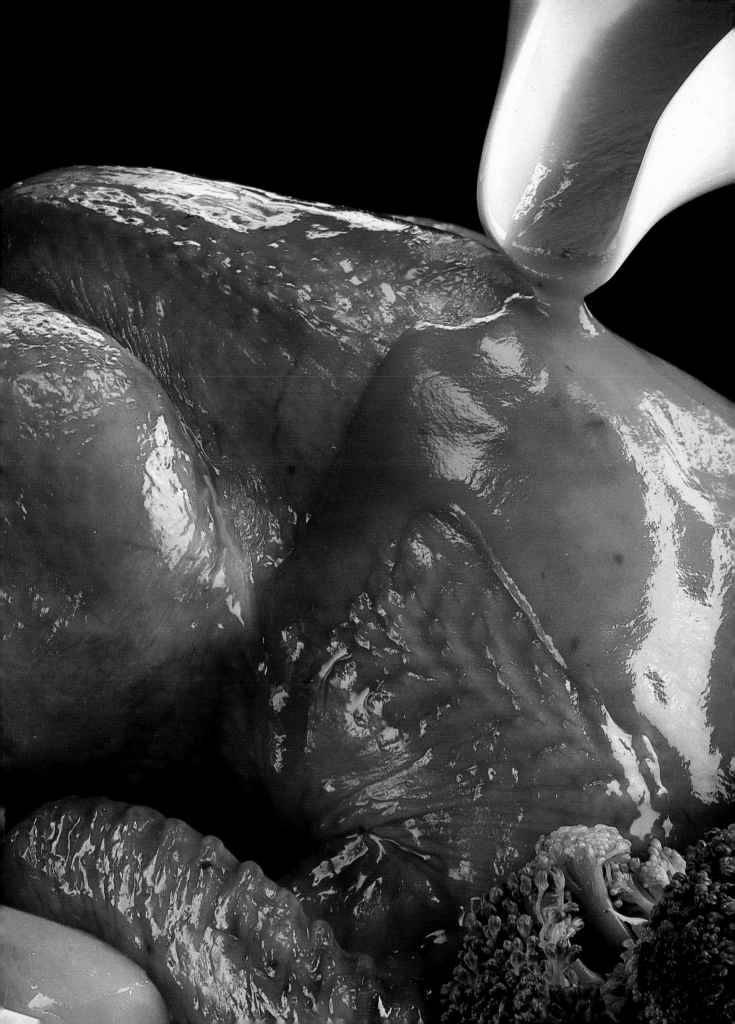

Vaucluse Sauce

Ingredients
30 mL (2 tablespoons) butter
30 mL (2 tablespoons) flour
375 mL (1-1/2 cups) 18% cream
625 mL (2-1/2 cups) hollandaise sauce (see basic recipe, page 12)
salt and pepper to taste

Method
— Put the butter in a dish and heat at 100% for 40 seconds; add the flour and mix well.
— Add the cream and cook at 100% for 4 to 5 minutes, stirring twice during the cooking time.
— Carefully add the hollandaise sauce, little by little, whisking continuously.
— Reduce the power level to 50% and heat through for 1 minute or until the sauce is hot, but do not allow it to boil. Beat with a whisk before serving.

Béchamel Sauce with Peppers

Ingredients
125 mL (1/2 cup) 18% cream
500 mL (2 cups) béchamel sauce (see basic recipe, page 13)
15 mL (1 tablespoon) red pepper, finely chopped
15 mL (1 tablespoon) green pepper, finely chopped
15 mL (1 tablespoon) yellow pepper, finely chopped

Method
— Add the cream to the béchamel sauce and mix well.
— Heat at 100% for 1 to 2 minutes, stirring once during the cooking time.
— Add the chopped peppers and serve.

Bread Sauce

Ingredients
1 small onion, whole
2 cloves
250 mL (1 cup) milk
pinch cayenne
300 mL (1-1/4 cups) breadcrumbs
15 mL (1 tablespoon) 35% cream
15 mL (1 tablespoon) butter
salt and pepper to taste

Method
— Stud the onion with the cloves.
— Pour the milk into a dish and add the onion and the cayenne.
— Leave the dish uncovered and cook at 100% for 3 to 4 minutes, stirring once.
— Add the breadcrumbs.
— Leave uncovered and cook at 100% for 2 to 3 minutes longer.
— Remove the onion and add the cream and butter.
— Beat with a whisk and season to taste before serving.

Chicken Velouté Sauce

Ingredients
60 mL (4 tablespoons) butter
30 mL (2 tablespoons) mushrooms, chopped
60 mL (4 tablespoons) flour
500 mL (2 cups) chicken stock
15 mL (1 tablespoon) lemon juice
50 mL (1/4 cup) 35% cream
5 mL (1 teaspoon) coriander

Method
— Put the butter in a dish and heat at 100% for 30 seconds.
— Add the mushrooms; cover and cook at 100% for 1 minute.
— Add the flour and mix well.
— Add the chicken stock and beat with a whisk.
— Cook at 100% for 5 to 7 minutes, stirring twice.
— Strain through a sieve and add the lemon juice, cream and coriander.
— Season to taste and heat at 100% for 1 minute before serving.

Curry Sauce

Ingredients
125 mL (1/2 cup) coconut, grated
250 mL (1 cup) coconut milk
1 apple
50 mL (1/4 cup) butter
2 onions, finely chopped
2 tomatoes, peeled and coarsely chopped
15 mL (1 tablespoon) curry powder
250 mL (1 cup) white wine
salt and pepper to taste

Method
— Combine the grated coconut with the coconut milk and let stand for 30 minutes.
— Peel and core the apple and cut it into quarters.
— Put the butter in a dish and heat at 100% for 1 minute; add the onions, cover and cook at 100% for 3 to 4 minutes, stirring halfway through the cooking time.
— Add the tomatoes, apple and curry powder and cook at 100% for 4 minutes, stirring halfway through the cooking time.
— Add the white wine and the coconut mixture.
— Cook at 100% for 3 minutes, stirring halfway through the cooking time.
— Pour the mixture into a blender and purée at high speed.
— Check the seasoning and adjust if necessary.
— Cook the puréed sauce at 100% for 2 to 3 minutes, stirring once.

Cranberry Sauce

Ingredients
500 mL (2 cups) cranberries
250 mL (1 cup) pears, grated
1 clove
pinch allspice
175 mL (3/4 cup) sugar
50 mL (1/4 cup) port
50 mL (1/4 cup) water
15 mL (1 tablespoon) lemon juice

Method
— Combine all the ingredients in a dish and mix well.
— Cover and cook at 100% for 10 minutes, stirring halfway through the cooking time.
— Strain through a sieve and chill in the refrigerator before serving.

MICROTIPS

The Proper Way To Defrost Chicken

To defrost chicken, whether an entire bird or one cut into pieces, place it on a rack or on an upside-down plate in a larger dish in the microwave oven. Arrange it so that the thicker parts are toward the outside of the dish and the thinner parts are toward the center, where the microwaves are less intense. To ensure that the meat defrosts evenly, shield the thinner parts such as the wings and the tips of the legs with aluminum foil, taking care to put the shiny side next to the meat.

Divide the defrosting time into several cycles. Give the dish a quarter-turn between each so that all parts of the bird are equally exposed to the microwaves.

If the bird is still frozen on the inside at the end of the defrosting period, run cold water from the tap into the body cavity. You will then be able to remove the giblets easily.

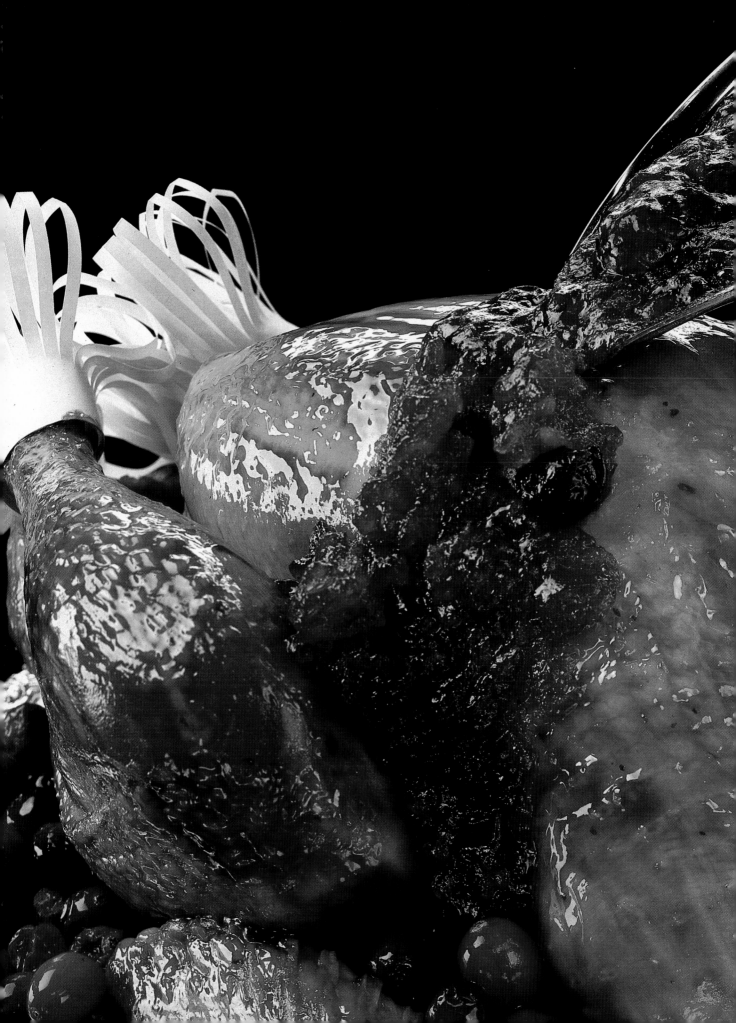

Madeira Sauce

Ingredients
50 mL (1/4 cup) Madeira wine
75 mL (1/3 cup) water
125 mL (1/2 cup) celery, finely chopped
125 mL (1/2 cup) carrot, grated
125 mL (1/2 cup) onion, finely chopped
375 mL (1-1/2 cups) beef consommé
1 mL (1/4 teaspoon) thyme
1 mL (1/4 teaspoon) savory
45 mL (3 tablespoons) butter
45 mL (3 tablespoons) flour

Method
— Put the water in a dish and add the celery, carrot and onion.
— Cook at 100% for 4 to 5 minutes, stirring once during the cooking time.
— Purée the vegetables in a blender along with a little of the beef consommé.
— Add the remaining consommé, the Madeira and the spices to the purée and set aside.
— Heat the butter at 100% for 1 minute, add the flour and mix well.
— Add the vegetable mixture to the flour and butter and beat with a whisk.
— Cook at 100% for 5 to 7 minutes or until the sauce thickens, stirring twice during the cooking time.

Deviled Sauce

Ingredients
45 mL (3 tablespoons) cornstarch, dissolved in 90 mL (6 tablespoons) cold water
500 mL (2 cups) beef consommé
15 mL (1 tablespoon) butter
4 green onions, finely sliced
250 mL (1 cup) white wine
pepper to taste

Method
— Add the dissolved cornstarch paste to the beef consommé and mix well.
— Cook at 100% for 6 to 7 minutes or until the mixture thickens, beating with a whisk twice during the cooking time, and set aside.
— Put the butter and green onions in a dish and cook at 100% for 2 to 3 minutes, stirring halfway through the cooking time.
— Add the white wine, leave uncovered, and cook at 100% for 5 minutes, stirring twice during the cooking time.
— Combine the two mixtures, reduce the power level to 70% and cook for 2 minutes, stirring once during the cooking time.

MICROTIPS

A Special Deglazing Technique

Whenever you fry, broil or roast meat, poultry, fish or seafood you will find that the cooking juices collect in the bottom of the pan and sometimes caramelize. You can loosen the juice by using a variety of liquids, such as those described in the Microtip on page 14. The best approach is to add just a little liquid to the pan, heat it over a moderate heat and scrape the pan with a utensil that won't cause scratches, such as a wooden spoon, to lift the caramelized juices.

Another tip—if you want to make your sauce extra special, add finely chopped vegetables to the pan before you add the liquid and sauté them briefly in the pan drippings. The combination of the caramelized juices and the lightly cooked vegetables produces sauces that are highly successful.

In Praise of Vegetables

Vegetables are all too frequently denied the treatment they deserve. There is no justification for this neglect; they are attractive, tasty and nutritious. A number of sauces can easily be prepared in the microwave oven to add a little style to your vegetables.

Given proper treatment in the microwave you need have no fear that sauces will stick to the pan or go lumpy, so it really is not difficult to prepare them. In fact, because many sauces improve when they are made ahead of time, you can do just that and either refrigerate or freeze them. Your microwave can be used to reheat them in next to no time.

On the following pages you will find some marvellous recipes for basic sauces to go with vegetables and you can have fun making variations. For example, changes in the Sour Cream Sauce may easily be made by adding different seasonings. Several sauces are based on roux: Sauce Bâtarde being one example and Polonaise Sauce, another. Variations on them may be made with the addition of cream, lemon juice, stock, aromatic herbs, spices and butter.

Hollandaise Sauce is the basis for Chantilly Sauce, an impressive classic to be served on special occasions.

There are also a number of sauces intended for use with meat, poultry, fish and seafood that can be successfully served with vegetables. Examples include Hollandaise Sauce, Béarnaise Sauce, Soubise Sauce, Mornay Sauce and Parsley Sauce, the recipes for which are offered in the preceding sections. It is a good idea to learn to distinguish between the delicately flavored sauces such as Hollandaise and Béarnaise, which go well with vegetables and delicately flavored meats, and the more strongly flavored sauces such as Mornay, Polonaise and Raisin Sauce, which can be served with a wide range of foods, including those with a very pronounced flavor.

And finally, don't forget that the vegetables themselves are especially conducive to microwave cooking; they retain all their natural flavor and color and are unlikely to go mushy. Try combining them with some of the sauces that follow, which will put them in a class of their own—and don't hesitate to make them the focus of your meal!

Lemon Butter Sauce

Ingredients
125 mL (1/2 cup) butter
15 mL (1 tablespoon) lemon zest, grated
30 mL (2 tablespoons) lemon juice
15 mL (1 tablespoon) dried parsley
pinch cayenne
2 drops Tabasco

Method
— Put the butter in a dish and heat at 100% for 2 minutes.
— Add all the other ingredients and mix well until smooth.
— Heat at 100% for 30 to 40 seconds.

Sour Cream Sauce

Ingredients
250 mL (1 cup) sour cream
2 mL (1/2 teaspoon) curry powder
15 mL (1 tablespoon) lemon juice
zest of 1 lemon
salt and pepper to taste

Method
— Combine all the ingredients in a bowl and mix well.
— Leave uncovered and cook at 70% for 2 to 3 minutes, stirring every minute.

Sauce Bâtarde

Ingredients
30 mL (2 tablespoons) butter
30 mL (2 tablespoons) flour
250 mL (1 cup) water
2 egg yolks
125 mL (1/2 cup) 35% cream
15 mL (1 tablespoon) lemon juice

Method
— Put the butter in a dish and heat at 100% for 30 seconds; add the flour and mix well.
— Add the water and cook at 100% for 4 to 5 minutes or until the mixture thickens.
— Beat the egg yolks with the cream and add a little of the hot sauce to the mixture.
— When the mixture is perfectly smooth, add the remaining hot sauce, whisking continuously.
— Add the lemon juice and whisk well.
— Heat at 100% for 1 to 2 minutes, stirring halfway through the cooking time. Do no allow the sauce to boil.

Hollandaise Chantilly Sauce

Ingredients
625 mL (2-1/2 cups) hollandaise sauce (see basic recipe, page 12)
125 mL (1/2 cup) 35% cream
salt and pepper to taste

Method
— Pour the hollandaise sauce into a bowl; chill for 15 minutes in the refrigerator if necessary.
— Whip the cream until it stands up in peaks.
— Fold the cream into the hollandaise sauce and mix well.
— Season to taste before serving.

Polonaise Sauce

Ingredients
45 mL (3 tablespoons) butter
45 mL (3 tablespoons) flour
375 mL (1-1/2 cups) veal stock
50 mL (1/4 cup) 35% cream
15 mL (1 tablespoon) lemon juice
125 mL (1/2 cup) sour cream
15 mL (1 tablespoon) horseradish
30 mL (2 tablespoons) fennel, chopped
salt and pepper to taste

Method
— Put the butter in a dish and heat at 100% for 40 seconds; add the flour and mix well.
— Add the veal stock, mix well and cook at 100% for 4 to 5 minutes or until the mixture thickens, stirring twice during the cooking time.
— Add the cream and lemon juice and cook at 100% for 1 minute.
— Add the remaining ingredients and mix well with a whisk.
— Reheat the sauce at 100% for 1 minute, but do not allow it to boil.
— Check the seasoning before serving and adjust if necessary.

Rosy Sauce

Ingredients
125 mL (1/2 cup) mayonnaise
50 mL (1/4 cup) ketchup
50 mL (1/4 cup) green onions, finely sliced
pepper to taste

Method
— Combine all the ingredients in a bowl and mix well, until perfectly smooth.
— Chill in the refrigerator for 2 hours.
— Just before serving, heat at 30% for 1 minute, stirring once.

MICROTIPS

To Rescue Sauces

Your mayonnaise is more likely to be successful if all the ingredients are at room temperature. When you add the oil to the egg yolks, do so *very slowly* at first, gradually increasing this addition to a steady thin stream. If, however, the mayonnaise starts to separate it can be rescued; simply beat another egg yolk and add the separated mixture to it just as slowly as you would the oil. The resulting mayonnaise should be smooth and velvety.

Although it is very easy to make béchamel sauce or any other sauce based on roux in the microwave, you must be careful to whisk it frequently or you may end up with lumps. Any lumps can usually be dealt with by beating the sauce vigorously with a wire whisk for a minute or two. If this technique doesn't work, you can either sieve the sauce or mix it in the blender.

Sauces based on egg yolks will curdle if you let them boil. A hollandaise sauce may do so if it is cooked at too high a power level. If it begins to separate take it out of the oven, add a tablespoon of cold water, mix well and allow it to cool. If it remains separated, whisk one teaspoon of lemon juice with one tablespoon of the hollandaise sauce until the mixture is perfectly smooth and creamy. Repeat this procedure, adding one tablespoon of the separated hollandaise at a time, making sure that the mixture is perfectly smooth before you add the next spoonful.

These rescue procedures are very time consuming; it is therefore better to avoid the problem by checking the sauce frequently during the cooking time and stirring it often. If the sauce is very hot when you take it out of the oven, set the dish in cold water immediately so that the sauce does not continue to cook.

Sauces To Bring Pasta to Life

Pasta is associated with Italian cooking, but in fact it has been a favorite in China for much longer. Today, however, it has become an international food and is popular all over the world.

Pasta is an economical staple but never dull. With its intriguing shapes, colors and multitude of traditional recipes, you need never tire of pasta. It can be served as an appetizer, main course or as an accompaniment to other dishes. You can enjoy it plain, stuffed, in soups and salads, hot or cold, with vegetables or with meat, fish or seafood. And, of course, how often is pasta served with sauce?

Pasta comes in all the colors of the rainbow. Basic pasta is pale yellow in color but it can also be made or bought in shades of orange, pink, dusky green, deep yellow and speckled green. The ingredients that lend these exotic colors to pasta are tomatoes, beets, spinach, saffron and fine herbs, respectively.

Although it takes roughly the same time to cook pasta in the microwave as it does to cook it in the conventional manner, the microwave is a real boon in making sauces for it easily and quickly. In many cases it is a good idea to make sauces for pasta in advance to allow the flavors to develop, and the microwave is a real asset when it comes to reheating them.

Pasta can be served very simply with olive oil, butter or cream and aromatic herbs and spices. However, there are two types of sauces that are commonly served with pasta, namely, sauces based on béchamel and variations on Tomato Sauce. On the following pages, you will find that olive oil and garlic are used quite frequently in the sauces for pasta, following the traditions of the French region of Provence as well as Italy. You will also find that onion, aromatic herbs and spices, tomatoes, cream and cheese are common ingredients, used time and time again. On occasion, meat, seafood, vegetables, eggs and offal are added to pasta sauces in order to create distinctive dishes.

Once again, you will find it easy to learn the basic principles of a good pasta sauce and in no time at all you will be developing your own recipes and converting old favorites to the microwave method.

Tomato Sauce

Ingredients

1 398 mL (14 oz) can tomatoes, crushed
75 mL (1/3 cup) tomato paste
30 mL (2 tablespoons) olive oil
4 cloves garlic, crushed
125 mL (1/2 cup) onion, chopped
5 mL (1 teaspoon) sugar
7 mL (1-1/2 teaspoons) oregano
5 mL (1 teaspoon) salt
2 mL (1/2 teaspoon) basil
1 bay leaf
pepper to taste

Method
— Cook the oil, garlic and onion at 100%
  for 3 to 4 minutes, stirring once.
— Add all the other ingredients and mix
  well.
— Cook at 100% for 4 to 6 minutes,
  stirring once during the cooking time.
  Remove the bay leaf before serving.

Anchovy Sauce

Ingredients

60 g (2 oz) anchovy fillets, drained and
chopped
50 mL (1/4 cup) oil
2 cloves garlic, cut into two
15 mL (1 tablespoon) dried parsley
30 mL (2 tablespoons) Parmesan cheese,
grated
5 mL (1 teaspoon) lemon juice

Method
— Pour the oil into a dish and add the
  garlic; cook at 100% for 2 to 3 minutes.
— Remove the garlic and discard; add all
  the other ingredients and mix well until
  smooth.

Spinach Sauce

Ingredients
284 g (10 oz) spinach, finely chopped
50 mL (1/4 cup) butter
5 mL (1 teaspoon) salt
250 mL (1 cup) ricotta cheese
50 mL (1/4 cup) Parmesan cheese, grated
50 mL (1/4 cup) milk
2 mL (1/2 teaspoon) nutmeg

Method
— Put the butter in a dish and heat at
  100% for 1 minute.
— Add the spinach, cover and cook at
  100% for 4 to 5 minutes, stirring once
  during the cooking time.
— Add all the other ingredients and mix
  well. For an even creamier sauce, purée
  the mixture in a blender at high speed
  for a few seconds.
— Reduce the power level to 70% and heat
  through for 1 to 2 minutes, stirring
  once.

Mariana Sauce

Ingredients
30 mL (2 tablespoon) oil
2 cloves garlic, crushed
1 onion, finely chopped
1 398 mL (14 oz) can tomatoes, crushed
1 156 mL (5-1/2 oz) can tomato paste
15 mL (1 tablespoon) sugar
2 mL (1/2 teaspoon) basil
salt to taste

Method
— Put the oil, garlic and onion in a dish
  and cook at 100% for 2 to 3 minutes,
  stirring once during the cooking time.
— Add all the other ingredients and mix
  well until they are smoothly blended.
— Leave uncovered and cook at 100% for
  10 to 12 minutes, stirring 3 times during
  the cooking time.

Clam Sauce

Ingredients
2 375 mL (12.5 oz) cans clams, in their
liquid
50 mL (1/4 cup) oil
2 cloves garlic, chopped
50 mL (1/4 cup) fresh parsley, chopped
50 mL (1/4 cup) white wine
5 mL (1 teaspoon) basil
salt and pepper to taste

Method
— Drain the clams and set the liquid aside.
— Pour the oil into a dish and add the
  garlic; cook at 100% for 2 to 3 minutes,
  stirring once during the cooking time.
— Add the parsley, white wine, seasoning
  and the clam liquid; cook at 100% for 4
  to 5 minutes, stirring halfway through
  the cooking time.
— Add the clams and heat at 100% for 2
  to 3 minutes, stirring once during the
  cooking time.

Pesto

Ingredients
3 cloves garlic, finely chopped
36 fresh basil leaves, finely chopped
coarse salt to taste
90 g (3 oz) Romano cheese, grated
at least 15 mL (1 tablespoon) olive oil, or
more if desired

Method
— Put a little of the garlic and a few basil
  leaves in a mortar and pound vigorously
  together with a little coarse salt.
— When the ingredients form a smooth
  paste, add a little more garlic and more
  basil leaves.
— Pound once more until these ingredients
  have been reduced to a paste; do not be
  tempted to add more ingredients until
  you have reached this stage.
— Continue this process until all the garlic
  and basil leaves are crushed; then add
  the Romano cheese and mix well to
  form a smooth thick paste.
— Add the olive oil to thin the paste to
  the desired consistency.

MICROTIPS

Cooking and Reheating Pasta

The actual cooking times for pasta obviously vary with the size, shape and quantity selected. Fresh pasta needs about half the time or less than that required for dried pasta. However, in general terms, cooking and reheating times for pasta are roughly the same for both microwave and conventional methods. It is therefore a good idea to make double quantities of a recipe and freeze half.

Always ensure that the water is boiling before you add the pasta and keep the power level the same throughout the cooking period. Ensure that the pasta is completely covered with water, otherwise it will not cook evenly. It is wise to cover the dish so that the water does not evaporate and to stir the pasta frequently during the cooking. When the pasta is cooked, rinse it under cold water to remove excess starch and to stop the cooking, and then drain well. Add a little oil or butter so that the pasta can

be reheated without sticking.

A number of pasta dishes as well as sauces for them are better if made in advance so that the flavors have time to combine and develop. Lasagna, meat sauce and tomato sauce fall into this category. Keep the assembled pasta dish or sauce in a microwave-safe container, preferably a round one, which will allow for even cooking or reheating. It is also a good idea to cover the dish for cooking or reheating to prevent it from drying out.

Sauces To Honor Meat

Meat is central to many Canadian meals. The first pioneers had to fortify themselves to deal with hard, physical labor in a harsh climate and so they needed a diet that was rich in protein. Meat has kept its place in Canadian culinary traditions even though lifestyles have long since changed for very many people. Our thriving meat industry produces an unlimited number of meat products for us to choose from.

As well, meat can be served with a number of sauces to provide even more variety. Sauces for meat typically include fat such as butter or oil, liquid such as the cooking juices and/or stock and a thickening agent such as flour, cream or egg yolks. Aromatic herbs and spices, vegetable juices and vegetable purées, wine and spirits and a range of commercial sauces and condiments such as soy sauce, Tabasco sauce and mustard may all be added to sauces for meat for variety in flavor, color and texture.

On the following pages you will find a range of sauces, all belonging to different types of meat. Traditional Brown Sauce, for example, is a great complement to beef and pork. It is basically made with onions that are cooked in butter, sprinkled with flour as a thickener and rich brown stock, but different aromatics may be added to vary the taste. Pepper Sauce, on the other hand, is made from a roux base, with heavy cream, brandy and peppercorns, a sauce that is perfect with grilled beef.

Raisin Sauce, Barbecue Sauce and many sweet and sour sauces tend to have cornstarch as a thickening agent. Raisin Sauce, which is a rather sweet sauce, goes well with veal or ham whereas Barbecue Sauce, which is more piquant, is better with beef, pork or poultry. Italian Sauce is thick and strongly flavored and best when made in advance. It is very versatile and is frequently associated with beef, pork and poultry.

Fennel Sauce, on the other hand, has a delicate, lemony flavor that complements such white meats as veal escallops and poached boneless chicken breasts.

Serve Teriyaki Sauce with broiled beef or pork. The combination of ginger and garlic in this sauce is bound to be a hit with your guests.

Fennel Sauce

Ingredients
7 mL (1-1/2 teaspoons) fresh fennel, chopped
60 mL (4 tablespoons) butter
60 mL (4 tablespoons) flour
15 mL (1 tablespoon) powdered chicken concentrate
5 mL (1 teaspoon) salt
500 mL (2 cups) chicken stock
50 mL (1/4 cup) lemon juice

Method
— Put the butter in a dish and heat at 100% for 2 to 3 minutes.
— Add the flour, powdered chicken concentrate, fennel and salt and mix well.
— Add the chicken stock and mix well until smooth.
— Cook at 100% for 4 to 6 minutes or until the mixture reaches the boiling point and thickens, stirring every 2 minutes.
— Add the lemon juice just before serving.

Brown Sauce

Ingredients
45 mL (3 tablespoons) butter
2 mL (1/2 teaspoon) sugar
1 onion, chopped
30 mL (2 tablespoons) flour
1 284 mL (10 oz) can beef consommé
pinch thyme
50 mL (1/4 cup) milk
1 bay leaf
125 mL (1/2 cup) powdered milk
50 mL (1/4 cup) water
15 mL (1 tablespoon) tomato paste

Method
— Put the butter in a dish, heat at 100% for 1 minute and add the sugar and onion; cover and cook at 100% for 2 to 3 minutes.
— Sprinkle with the flour and mix well.
— Add the consommé, thyme, milk and bay leaf and cook at 100% for 2 minutes, stirring once.
— Dissolve the powdered milk in the water and add it to the sauce along with the tomato paste; cook at 100% for 2 to 3 minutes, stirring every minute.

Barbecue Sauce

Ingredients
50 mL (1/4 cup) onion, grated
15 mL (1 tablespoon) cornstarch
30 mL (2 tablespoons) cold water
125 mL (1/2 cup) vegetable juice
30 mL (2 tablespoons) brown sugar
15 mL (1 tablespoon) Worcestershire sauce
2 drops Tabasco

Method
— Put the onion in a dish and cook at 100% for 2 minutes, stirring once during the cooking time.
— Dissolve the cornstarch in the water and add it to the dish along with the remaining ingredients.
— Cook at 100% for 2 to 3 minutes, stirring every minute, until the mixture thickens.

Peppercorn Sauce

Ingredients
12 peppercorns, coarsely crushed
30 mL (2 tablespoons) butter
15 mL (1 tablespoon) flour, toasted
125 mL (1/2 cup) 35% cream
30 mL (2 tablespoons) brandy
freshly ground pepper

Method
— Put the butter in a dish and melt at 100% for 40 seconds; add the flour and mix well.
— Add the remaining ingredients; mix well and cook at 100% for 1 to 2 minutes or until the sauce thickens, stirring after 40 seconds. Strain and serve.

Italian Sauce

Ingredients
2 onions, chopped
2 cloves garlic, chopped
450 g (1 lb) ground beef
225 g (1/2 lb) ground veal
225 g (1/2 lb) ground pork
1 1.5 L (48 oz) can tomato juice
1 213 mL (7.5 oz) can tomato paste
1 540 mL (19 oz) can tomato soup
1 796 mL (28 oz) can tomatoes, chopped
garlic salt
pepper to taste
pinch sugar
2 bay leaves
oregano, basil, thyme and chili powder to taste
500 mL (2 cups) celery, chopped

Method
— Cook the onion and garlic at 100% for 3 minutes.
— Add all the meat and cook at 100% for 5 to 8 minutes, stirring every 2 minutes during the cooking time.
— Add the tomato juice, paste, soup and the canned tomatoes and mix well; then add all the seasoning.
— Cook at 100% for 40 minutes and then add the celery.
— Continue to cook at 100% for 30 minutes and check the consistency of the sauce. If you want it thicker, continue to cook for periods of 15 minutes at a time, until it is as you want it.
— Remove bay leaves before serving.

Teriyaki Sauce

Ingredients
50 mL (1/4 cup) oil
2 cloves garlic, crushed
30 mL (2 tablespoons) soy sauce
10 mL (2 teaspoons) ginger
5 mL (1 teaspoon) sugar

Method
— Put the oil and garlic in a dish and cook at 100% for 2 minutes.
— Add all the other ingredients and mix well.
— Allow to stand for 30 minutes at room temperature before serving.

MICROTIPS
Hints for Successful Sauces
The cooking times for sauces can vary considerably, depending on the temperature of the ingredients used at the start of cooking. For example, if cold milk is added to the roux when making a béchamel, the sauce will obviously take longer to cook than if hot milk had been used. Such factors should be taken into consideration when determining your cooking times.

It is easier to stir sauce if you make it in a bowl or a round dish and it will also cook more evenly in the microwave oven. Use a whisk to stir and beat the sauce as it cooks to make it smooth and velvety.

When a recipe calls for cornstarch as a thickening agent it should always be dissolved in a little cold liquid first and then stirred until a smooth, thin paste is obtained. It may then be added to the hot sauce.

If you want to reduce a sauce or to thicken it without the addition of flour, cook it at 100% for one minute at a time, stirring at the end of each minute. Repeat this procedure until the sauce has the desired consistency.

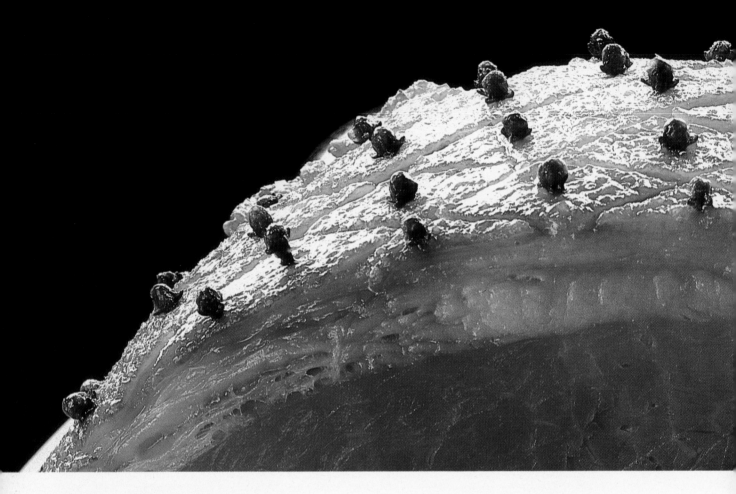

Amazing Glazes

Ham must surely be one of the most popular types of meat in North America. It makes a marvellous buffet centerpiece—with its surface cut into a neat diamond pattern and studded with cloves and fruit and surrounded with other colorful party offerings to complete the effect. Eye-catching as it is, this ham can be easily upstaged by one that is properly glazed, with a soft amber glow. Even those who don't particularly appreciate the taste of ham would agree that prepared in this way ham really looks good.

Glazing ham is a technique found in many culinary traditions. As you probably know, this procedure normally involves basting the ham, as it cooks, with stock that has been well reduced or some other syrup-like liquid, and the glaze forms a very thin but shiny coating on the surface.

Traditionally, glazes were made with a salty or sweet mixture that was applied to the ham and then caramelized at a high temperature at the end of the cooking time. These glazes were frequently based on brown stock that had been reduced and filtered several times. Fruit and fruit juices and syrups, icing sugar, brown sugar, and heavy syrups such as molasses were, and still are, sometimes added.

Glazing done in the microwave oven, however, requires a somewhat modified technique. Instead of caramelizing sugar quickly at a high temperature, the microwave cooks the glaze over a longer period of time and at a lower temperature. Nevertheless, the overall cooking time is still shorter. The recipe on page 53, opposite, demonstrates this technique, the results of which are bound to impress your guests.

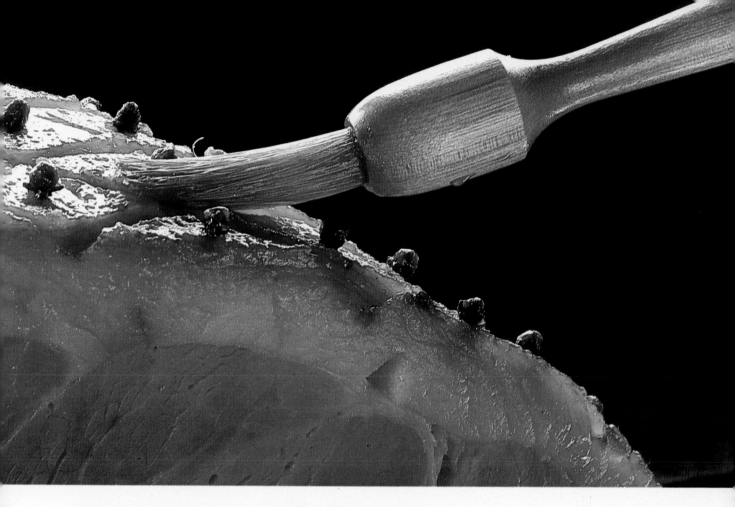

Glazed Ham with Peaches

Ingredients
1 boneless ham, 1.8 kg (4 lb), cut from the
leg
50 mL (1/4 cup) peach syrup
250 mL (1 cup) brown sugar
30 mL (2 tablespoons) vinegar
2 mL (1/2 teaspoon) cloves
1 mL (1/4 teaspoon) cinnamon
1 796 mL (28 oz) can peach halves
paprika to taste
125 mL (1/2 cup) hot water

Method
— Make a glaze by combining the peach
   syrup, brown sugar, vinegar, cloves and
   cinnamon. Mix well.
— Dry the peach halves and arrange them
   in a dish; sprinkle with paprika and a
   little of the glaze.
— Lay the ham on the peaches, fat side
   down, and add the hot water; cover and
   cook at 50% for 20 minutes.
— Give the dish a half-turn; cook at 50%
   for another 20 minutes.
— Remove the ham and make diagonal
   cuts to create a diamond pattern on the
   surface and baste with the glaze. Put
   back in the dish, fat side up, and cover
   and cook at 50% for 20 minutes.
— Baste the ham with the glaze once again
   and continue to cook at 50% for 20
   minutes.
— Repeat the glazing process and continue
   to cook at 50% for 20 minutes or until
   the meat is tender.

Raisin Sauce

Ingredients
125 mL (1/2 cup) raisins
125 mL (1/2 cup) water
75 mL (1/3 cup) redcurrant jelly
pinch allspice
15 mL (1 tablespoon) cornstarch
75 mL (1/3 cup) orange juice

Method
— Combine the raisins, water, redcurrant jelly and allspice in a dish and mix well.
— Cook at 100% for 2 minutes.
— Dissolve the cornstarch in the orange juice and stir into the sauce.
— Cook at 100% for 1 to 2 minutes, stirring once during the cooking time.

Applesauce

Ingredients
5 apples
60 mL (4 tablespoons) apple juice
30 mL (2 tablespoons) butter
30 mL (2 tablespoons) kirsh

Method
— Peel and core the apples and cut into pieces.
— Arrange the apple pieces in a dish and add the apple juice.
— Cover and cook at 100% for 4 to 5 minutes.
— Purée the mixture at high speed in a blender for a few seconds.
— Add the butter and kirsch and mix well before serving.

MICROTIPS

Add a Little Zest to Your Sauces

One very easy way to make your sauce more tasty is with the use of chicken skin. Remove the skin from cooked chicken, add it to your sauce, cook for about 2 minutes in the microwave oven and remove the skin before serving.

If you find your tomato sauce too sharp try adding a little sugar, which tones down the acidity inherent in tomatoes and tomato products.

Some herbs lose their flavor when they are cooked. Examples include chives, chervil and parsley. To retain their distinctive flavor, add them at the last minute when the sauce is just about cooked.

You can vary the flavor of soups and sauces by using different herbs in your bouquet garni. The three traditional herbs include parsley, thyme and bay leaves. Try using rosemary, savory, tarragon or even orange zest in place of thyme—or in addition to it.

Sauces can be kept in the freezer for several months. Many reheated sauces tend to have a better flavor than those freshly made. It is therefore a good idea to make a large batch of sauce and freeze it in microwave-safe dishes in portions appropriate for later use.

Soup, Beautiful Soup

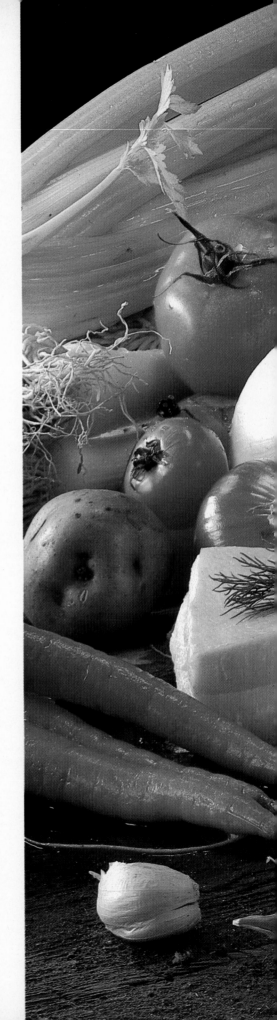

Soups are wonderful starters for any meal and some are meals in themselves. There are many categories of soup and they can be classified according to their consistency.

Clear soups are made with stock that has been concentrated (or reduced) to a great extent, as in a consommé, or to a lesser extent, as in broths or bouillons. Broths or bouillons may be served as light clear soups or may constitute the base of soups containing many other ingredients, known as compound broths.

Compound broths contain a large number of different ingredients, all of which add flavor and texture. Vegetables are a common addition. They are cooked so that they remain slightly crisp for Oriental-style soups but may be cooked until soft for home-style soups. Poultry and meat are also frequent and flavorful ingredients. Some people prefer an even heartier broth, more of a meal in itself, and add grains and cereals to it. Barley is an example, which is featured in the well-known Scotch Broth.

Soups classified as thick soups may be puréed, cream or velouté soups. A puréed soup is made with stock but is thickened with vegetables that have been puréed or sieved. It provides a marvellous way to get children to eat vegetables they normally won't touch! Starchy ingredients such as potatoes and legumes are particularly useful for thickening puréed soups, although many other vegetables may be used as well.

Cream soups, as their name implies, are basically puréed soups with the addition of cream or, if you prefer, whole milk or even skim milk. Some people like these soups with a knob of butter, which enriches them.

A velouté soup is thickened with cream and egg yolks. It is often regarded as the aristocrat of soups, its consistency beautifully smooth and velvety, but it is really a cream soup that is extraordinarily rich. In fact, some people feel that the amount of fussing required to add the egg yolks properly, without having them curdle, is scarcely worth the trouble.

Bisques and chowders are soups made with fish and shellfish, one of the most popular being lobster bisque. However, this type of soup can be made with other shellfish, such as crab, shrimp and oysters, as well. A bisque is a creamy soup made with puréed shellfish and usually thickened with breadcrumbs.

Soups may be served hot in winter and cold in summer, and there are a thousand and one ways of making them. Because the majority of soups are based on one essential ingredient, stock, we offer recipes for four basic stocks on the pages that follow—irresistible incentives to get you started in the creation of great soups!

13 g
Persil
Les Fines Herbes de Chez Nous Inc.

11 g
Marjolaine
Les Fines Herbes de Chez N...

Meat Stock

Ingredients
450 g (1 lb) shin of beef
450 g (1 lb) chicken wings or necks
450 g (1 lb) shin of veal
2.5 L (10 cups) water
450 g (1 lb) carrots, sliced
1 onion, studded with 2 cloves
2 cloves garlic, cut into two
1 bouquet garni

Method
— Put all the ingredients into a 4 L
  (16 cup) casserole and stir.
— Cook uncovered at 100% for 30
  minutes and stir.
— Reduce the power level to 70% and
  cook uncovered for 2 hours, stirring
  and skimming the surface several times.
  For a stronger flavor, simmer for a little
  longer.
— Strain the stock and remove the fat
  from the surface.

Chicken Stock

Ingredients
1 chicken carcass
450 g (1 lb) chicken wings and necks
4 carrots, sliced
2 sticks celery, sliced
1 onion, chopped
2 bay leaves
15 mL (1 tablespoon) salt
12 peppercorns
15 mL (1 tablespoon) poultry seasoning
2 L (8 cups) water

Method
— Put all the ingredients into a 4 L
  (16 cup) casserole and stir.
— Cook uncovered at 100% for 30
  minutes.
— Skim the surface and stir.
— Reduce the power level to 70% and
  cook for 1 hour and 30 minutes; stir
  and skim twice during the cooking time.
— Strain the stock and remove the fat
  from the surface.

Vegetable Stock

Ingredients
2 leeks, finely sliced
2 sticks celery, finely sliced
4 carrots, finely sliced
125 mL (1/2 cup) celery leaves, chopped
2 onions, finely sliced
1 quarter cabbage, grated
50 mL (1/4 cup) fresh parsley
1.5 L (6 cups) water
1 bay leaf
salt to taste
5 mL (1 teaspoon) thyme

Method
— Put all the ingredients into a 4 L
  (16 cup) casserole and stir.
— Cook uncovered at 100% for 1 hour,
  skimming the surface and stirring twice
  during the cooking time.
— Strain the stock, without pressing the
  vegetables against the sides of the sieve.
— Leave to drain for 10 minutes.

Fish Stock

Ingredients
1.1 kg (2-1/2 lb) fish, including the heads,
bones, and trimmings
1 onion, finely sliced
1 leek, finely sliced
2 carrots, finely sliced
1 bouquet garni
2 L (8 cups) water
salt and pepper to taste

Method
— Put all the ingredients into a 4 L
  (16 cup) casserole and stir.
— Cook uncovered at 100% for 1 hour,
  skimming the surface and stirring the
  stock several times during the cooking.
— Strain the stock without applying any
  pressure to the solid ingredients.

Garnishes for Clear Soups

Visual appeal is very important when it comes to food presentation, and what better way to show off a perfectly clear soup or a consommé than with a delicate, clever or even whimsical garnish.

The simplest and in many cases the most delicate garnish is merely a touch of chopped fresh herbs such as chives, parsley, chervil or tarragon. Herbs are colorful and add just a hint of their distinctive flavor.

Vegetables, cut into fine julienne strips, a small dice or star shapes, also make an excellent garnish. Root vegetables such as carrots, potatoes and turnips may be cut into imaginative shapes and added to a lovely golden consommé to float around in a delightfully decorative manner. And leafy vegetables such as lettuce and spinach may be shredded and placed on the surface, like so many tiny feathers, for a lighter touch.

Bread is another frequent garnish for clear soups. It may be dried, toasted, crumbled, made into croutons, or cut into slices and topped with a poached egg or grated cheese—a very traditional garnish and a sure winner.

Pasta is used as a garnish for consommé the world over and is available in an unlimited number of shapes and colors. Tortellini and vermicelli add interest and a particularly pleasant texture.

Dumplings made with flour and eggs or potatoes, such as spaetzle or gnocchi, are also traditional and decorative garnishes for clear soups. An alternative is tiny meatballs.

You might also like to experiment with an Oriental-style garnish made with eggs. You simply beat an egg with a little flour and salt and add the mixture to the hot consommé. As you stir, it will form fine, floating threads, an extremely delicate garnish.

A beautiful clear soup or consommé featuring a distinctive garnish makes the perfect starter to an equally elegant meal.

Thick Soups

In days gone by, thick soups were served as meals in their own right, and they still sometimes are. What gives thick soups distinction and makes them different from others is that their ingredients are sieved or puréed and then blended with just enough of the basic cooking stock to yield a smooth, creamy consistency.

Soups that are based on starchy vegetables such as carrots or rutabagas or legumes such as lentils, peas and beans are the easiest to prepare. You need only select one or two such ingredients to give great flavor to your soup without worrying about its consistency. It is up to you to decide whether to leave a little texture in your soup or if your prefer to purée it until it is smooth. In either case, you should take care not to spoil the natural flavor of the ingredients by overcooking them.

Thick soups require fairly minimal preparation and they are not terribly complicated to make, but certain rules must be followed. For instance, some vegetables, such as leeks and celery, do not contain enough starch of their own to make a good thick soup. These vegetables, if puréed and added to stock, would tend to separate into tiny particles. It is therefore important to add a starchy ingredient, such as potatoes, to improve the consistency. Rice and other grains can also be added to act as thickening agents.

The addition of cream, whole milk or even skim milk to a puréed soup transforms it into a cream soup and with the use of a *liaison,* a mixture of heavy cream and egg yolks, it becomes a rich velouté.

Thick soups, whether puréed, cream or velouté, are enjoyable and intriguing to eat—and you can have fun asking your guests to speculate on the combination of ingredients used in their preparation.

Cream of Carrot Soup

Ingredients
1 kg (2 lb) carrots, grated
50 mL (1/4 cup) butter
1 onion, chopped
4 cloves garlic, crushed
1.75 L (7 cups) meat stock
125 mL (1/2 cup) 35% cream
10 mL (2 teaspoons) sugar
salt and pepper to taste
15 mL (1 tablespoon) parsley, chopped

Method
— Put the butter in a dish and heat at 100% for 1 minute.
— Add the onion, carrot and garlic and mix well; cover and cook at 100% for 4 to 5 minutes, stirring once.
— Add the stock, cover and continue to cook at 100% for 1 hour, stirring at least once.
— Purée in a blender, stir in the cream and sugar and season; sprinkle with parsley before serving.

NOTE: This soup can be thinned with more meat stock if necessary. It is usually served cold, but is equally good hot. To heat it in the microwave, set the power level at 70% and leave it for 5 to 7 minutes, or until heated through, stirring every minute.

MICROTIPS

Stocks and Their Evolution

It is always useful to have a good supply of stock on hand for making soups and sauces. Meat stock (made from veal, beef, lamb or pork), chicken stock and fumet (fish stock) can all be used as flavorful bases. Homemade stocks are vastly superior to those you obtain from cans or packages.

Stock can be kept for several months in the freezer. It can also be kept for three or four days in the refrigerator in a tightly sealed container. If you do keep it in the refrigerator, however, remember to boil it for a few minutes and skim the surface before using to remove any impurities and to prevent bacterial growth.

It is really quite easy to make chicken stock, or any other type for that matter. To make chicken stock, simply boil the chicken carcass, any meat trimmings and the giblets with vegetables, aromatic herbs and spices in a container that is not covered. Divide the cooking time into several shorter periods and, at the end of each, take the stock out of the oven and skim off any impurities that have risen to the surface. When the stock has reduced sufficiently and has a good, strong flavor, strain it and remove the fat.

Other ingredients may then be used with the resulting stock to make a simple soup or sauce. Roux may be used to thicken it and a duxelles, a mirepoix of chopped vegetables, brandy, wine or cream may be added. This approach is basic to the creation of any soup or sauce, depending on the type of stock used and the ingredients that are added.

Sauce Espagnole is the mother of all the brown sauces and Sauce Velouté, the mother of all blond sauces. More complex variants are based on these basic sauces—some including Sauce Poulette (with lemon and parsley), Caper Sauce, Breton Sauce (with vegetables and cream), Bordelaise Sauce, Bercy Sauce (with green onions), and Piquant Sauce. These sauces all may be served with a variety of foods, such as fish and shellfish, poultry, mushrooms, eggs, steak, pork chops, tongue and even kidney.

Cream of Cauliflower Soup

Ingredients
1 small cauliflower, finely sliced
625 mL (2-1/2 cups) chicken stock
1 potato, finely sliced
250 mL (1 cup) celery, finely sliced
1 bay leaf
pinch nutmeg
salt and pepper to taste
50 mL (1/4 cup) milk

Method
— Pour 250 mL (1 cup) of the chicken
  stock into a dish; add the cauliflower,
  potato, celery and bay leaf.
— Cover and cook at 100% for
  15 minutes, stirring once during the
  cooking time.
— Remove the bay leaf and purée in a
  blender at high speed for a few seconds.

— Strain through a sieve and add the
  remaining chicken stock and nutmeg;
  season with salt and pepper.
— Cover and cook at 100% for 4 to 6
  minutes, stirring once during the
  cooking time.
— Add the milk and mix well; check the
  seasoning before you serve the soup.

Purée of Pea Soup

Ingredients
900 g (2 lb) frozen peas
30 mL (2 tablespoons) butter
3 leeks, whites only, finely chopped
1 onion, finely chopped
30 mL (2 tablespoons) flour
1.75 L (7 cups) chicken stock
1 mint leaf
250 mL (1 cup) 18% cream
salt and pepper to taste

Method
— Put the butter in a large casserole and
  heat at 100% for 40 seconds.
— Add the leeks and onion; cover and
  cook at 100% for 4 to 5 minutes,
  stirring once during the cooking time.
— Sprinkle with the flour and mix well.
— Pour the chicken stock into the
  casserole; cover and bring to the boil by
  heating at 100% for 12 to 14 minutes.

— Add the mint and frozen peas; cover
  and cook at 100% for 12 to 14 minutes.
— Purée the mixture in a blender at high
  speed.
— Strain through a sieve into a dish and
  bring to the boil by heating at 100% for
  4 to 5 minutes.
— Add the cream, salt and pepper before
  serving. If the soup is too thick, you
  can thin it with a little milk.

Cream of Mushroom Soup

Ingredients
225 g (8 oz) mushrooms, finely sliced
4 large mushrooms, finely sliced
75 mL (5 tablespoons) butter
1 onion, finely chopped
750 mL (3 cups) water
45 mL (3 tablespoons) flour
250 mL (1 cup) 18% cream
salt and pepper to taste

Method
— Put 30 mL (2 tablespoons) of the butter in a dish and heat at 100% for 30 seconds.
— Add the 225 g (8 oz) mushrooms (not the large ones) and the onion; cover and cook at 100% for 3 to 4 minutes.
— Add the water; cover again and cook at 100% for 30 minutes, stirring once during the cooking time.
— Purée in a blender at high speed and set aside.
— Heat the remaining butter at 100% for 40 seconds; add the flour and mix well.
— Add the cream and beat with a whisk; cook at 100% for 3 to 4 minutes, stirring twice during the cooking time.
— Add the purée to the hot cream sauce, whisking constantly.
— Add the large mushroom slices and season; heat through at 100% for 3 to 4 minutes or until the mixture is hot, stirring once.

MICROTIPS

Testing Poultry for Doneness

You will naturally follow the guidelines given in your recipe when cooking poultry, but remember that it is good idea to periodically check the cooking progress. Individual birds vary in terms of size and age and overcooked meat is dry and tasteless. There are three methods you can use to test whether or not a bird is done.

One is to examine the color of the meat; poultry is done when both the white and dark meat have lost all traces of pink.

The second is to wiggle the thigh bone. If it moves easily or comes away from the bird, it means that the meat is cooked.

The third is to place a meat thermometer in the thickest part of the dark meat, taking care to avoid any contact with either fat or bone which conduct heat and would give a false reading. If the thermometer indicates that the meat has reached the recommended temperature, the bird is done.

Remember, however, that a conventional meat thermometer should never be used in the microwave oven. Some microwave models are equipped with a temperature probe, which is used in much the same way. These devices are very sophisticated; when the meat reaches the correct temperature the oven switches itself off.

Cream of Asparagus Soup

Ingredients
450 g (1 lb) asparagus
60 mL (4 tablespoons) butter
1 onion, finely chopped
75 mL (5 tablespoons) flour
1 L (4 cups) chicken stock
15 mL (1 tablespoon) chives
125 mL (1/2 cup) 18% cream
15 mL (1 tablespoon) lemon juice
2 mL (1/2 teaspoon) paprika
salt and pepper to taste

Method
— Remove the asparagus tips, setting some aside to use as a garnish. Chop the stalks.
— Put the butter in a dish and heat at 100% for 1 minute; add the onion and asparagus; cover and cook at 100% for 4 to 5 minutes.
— Add the flour, mix well, blend in the chicken stock and add the chives.
— Cover and cook at 100% for 10 minutes, stirring three times during the cooking.
— Purée the mixture at high speed in a blender.
— Add the cream, lemon juice and the seasonings.
— Heat through at 100% for 3 to 5 minutes, stirring once.
— Blanch the asparagus tips that have been set aside by cooking them at 100% for 2 minutes.
— Pour the soup into individual bowls and garnish each with an asparagus tip before serving.

MICROTIPS

White Roux: A Base for White Sauces

White roux, which is used to prepare a simple béchamel and other white sauces, can be made in the following way. Melt some butter, add an equal quantity of flour and mix well. Heat the mixture until it begins to foam slightly. Stir the roux frequently as it heats to prevent it from turning brown and to prevent lumps from forming. There is no reason to be nervous about opening the oven frequently to check the roux and to give it a stir.

When the roux begins to bubble slightly, take it out of the oven and allow it to cool. If the liquid to be used is heated in advance you will find it easier to make the sauce perfectly smooth when the liquid is added. Milk is usually used for béchamel sauce. Alternatives for other white sauces include white stock or fish stock with the addition of a little heavy cream. Or, white wine could be used in combination with the stock. The resulting sauce is suitable for serving with veal or fish.

The flavor of béchamel comes to life with the addition of an onion studded with cloves, a pinch of nutmeg, salt and pepper during its cooking. Be sure to strain it and add a little butter to enrich it before serving.

If a skin should form on the surface of a sauce, once it is cooked, pour a little melted butter on the sauce or put some plastic wrap directly on top.

Cream of Leek and Potato Soup

Ingredients
750 mL (3 cups) leeks, white parts only, chopped and firmly packed
1.5 L (6 cups) potatoes, cut into small cubes
1.5 L (6 cups) hot chicken stock
salt and pepper to taste
125 mL (1/2 cup) 18% cream
15 mL (1 tablespoon) lemon juice

Method
— Put the leeks and potatoes into a casserole with one third of the chicken stock; cover and cook at 100% for 15 to 18 minutes, stirring halfway through the cooking time.
— Purée the mixture at high speed in a blender, adding the remaining chicken stock gradually as you do.
— Add the salt, pepper, cream and lemon juice.
— Cook at 100% for 3 to 4 minutes, stirring once.

Cream of Cucumber and Artichoke Soup

Ingredients
2 cucumbers, peeled, seeded and chopped
6 artichoke hearts, cut into pieces
60 mL (4 tablespoons) butter
1 onion, finely sliced
1 stick celery, finely sliced
1 L (4 cups) chicken stock
250 mL (1 cup) milk
175 mL (3/4 cup) 18% cream
salt and pepper to taste
parsley, chopped

Method
— Put the butter in a dish and heat at 100% for 1 minute; add the cucumbers, artichoke hearts, onion and celery.
— Cover and cook at 100% for 3 minutes, stirring once during the cooking time.
— Add the chicken stock; cover again and cook at 100% for 12 to 15 minutes or until the vegetables are just done.
— Add the milk and cook at 100% for 3 minutes.
— Purée the mixture at high speed in a blender and then stir in the cream.
— Add salt and pepper to taste and heat through at 100% for 2 minutes.
— Garnish with parsley before serving.

MICROTIPS

Soups: Conventional Cooking or Microwave Method?

The microwave oven has had a considerable impact on our lifestyles and on the way we cook. The microwave method of making soup provides an obvious example.

We tend to think of preparing soup as first requiring the long, slow process of simmering stock. Then meat or chicken is poached very gently and vegetables are added and simmered over a low heat for a long period of time.

Soup prepared in the microwave oven involves less work and much less time. The stock itself can be made more quickly. The vegetables may be cooked separately in little or no water and then added to the stock shortly before the soup is to be served. The result is a really tasty soup in which the vegetables retain all their flavor and nutritional value. Whatever would great-grandmother say!

Neptune's Choice: Bisques and Bouillabaisse

Fish soups, clear or creamy, tend to be unpopular with children and even with some adults. But a good bisque has a wonderful velvety texture and a subtle, sophisticated taste. If your memories of this type of soup are unpleasant, you really must try it again; you are sure to discover just how wonderful it is.

The term "bisque" derives from the Basque Provinces on the shores of the Bay of Biscay and dates back to the fourteenth century. It refers to the traditional thick and creamy soups made from such puréed shellfish as oysters, lobster, shrimp and crabs, all so popular in that region. To this day, people tend to associate fish and seafood soups with the Mediterranean countries, where they have certainly been very popular.

Purists go to considerable lengths to achieve the perfect bisque. Some insist that the best bisque must be made with living sea creatures and that their shells, if crustacean, must be crushed and cooked with the soup and then sieved for the perfect flavor and color. However, a perfectly satisfactory variation can be prepared with fresh but not living shellfish. and without their shells.

Other fish soups are based on broth and, like compound broths, contain a number of ingredients with varying textures and flavors, including fish and the meat of mollusks and crustaceans. Bouillabaisse is probably the most well-known soup of this kind. It may contain fish, clams, mussels, scallops, lobster and shrimp, in any combination, depending on the recipe chosen. Whatever the ingredients, the taste of the fish blends harmoniously with that of tomato, an essential ingredient. As such, bouillabaisse is typical of Provençale cooking, which relies heavily on combinations of fish, tomatoes and herbs.

Clams and mussels are also used in soups known as chowders, notably clam chowder, which may be enriched with cream or milk along with herbs, green onions and parsley.

Fish soups not only have a truly distinctive flavor and aroma but are extremely healthy as well. Don't wait to try them on your guests; be a little daring and you'll likely make some very willing converts!

Seafood Chowder

Ingredients
175 g (6 oz) crabmeat
130 g (4-1/2 oz) shrimps
15 mL (1 tablespoon) butter
75 mL (1/3 cup) onion, finely chopped
50 mL (1/4 cup) carrot, grated
30 mL (2 tablespoons) celery, finely chopped
50 mL (1/4 cup) flour
1 mL (1/4 teaspoon) each salt, paprika, thyme and pepper
175 mL (3/4 cup) chicken stock
50 mL (1/4 cup) sherry
175 mL (3/4 cup) 18% cream

Method
— Put the butter, onion, carrot and celery in a dish and cook at 100% for 3 to 4 minutes.
— Add the flour, the seasoning, chicken stock and sherry, stirring constantly with each addition.
— Mix well and cook at 100% for 2 to 3 minutes or until the mixture thickens, stirring halfway through the cooking time.
— Add the cream and mix well; add the crabmeat and the shrimps, stirring gently.
— Reduce the power level to 90% and cook for 8 to 10 minutes, stirring every 2 minutes.

Cream of Lobster Soup

Ingredients
175 g (6 oz) lobster meat, cooked
60 mL (4 tablespoons) butter
3 green onions, finely sliced
30 mL (2 tablespoons) white wine
1 L (4 cups) chicken stock
50 mL (1/4 cup) 10% cream
2 egg whites, beaten until stiff
10 mL (2 teaspoons) cornstarch
30 mL (2 tablespoons) cold water
salt and pepper to taste

Method
— Put the butter in a dish and heat at 100% for 1 minute; add the green onions, lobster meat and wine.
— Cook at 100% for 2 minutes.
— Add the chicken stock and cook at 100% for 8 to 10 minutes, stirring twice during the cooking time.
— Mix the cream with the beaten egg whites very carefully and set aside.
— Dissolve the cornstarch in the water and stir into the cream and egg white mixture.
— Combine the two mixtures and cook at 100% for 4 to 6 minutes or until the soup thickens, stirring every 2 minutes.

MICROTIPS

An Easy Way To Cook Shrimps

The shrimps that you buy fresh and cook yourself have infinitely more flavor than those prepared commercially and they will greatly enhance the flavor of your bisques and seafood dishes. The best way to cook fresh jumbo shrimps is to simmer them in a court bouillon. Court bouillon, as described earlier in this volume, is a combination of water and wine, vinegar or lemon juice, in which herbs and aromatic vegetables such as onions and carrots are simmered. Strain the court bouillon and add the shrimps. Cook them until they turn a deep pink.

Allow them to cool in the liquid and then remove the shells, which will have softened considerably during the cooking process. Finally, make a shallow incision along each shrimp lengthwise and remove the black vein just under the flesh.

Cod Soup

Ingredients
900 g (2 lb) cod, cut into 2.5 cm (1 inch)
cubes
3 slices bacon, cut into four
1 onion, sliced
500 mL (2 cups) potatoes, finely sliced
375 mL (1-1/2 cups) water
500 mL (2 cups) milk
pinch savory
salt and pepper to taste

Method
— Put the bacon and onion in a casserole
and cook at 100% for 3 to 4 minutes or
until the bacon is crisp, stirring once
during the cooking time.
— Add the potatoes and cook at 100% for
4 minutes, stirring once.
— Arrange alternating layers of the potato
mixture and the cod in a 4 L (16 cup)
casserole and add the water; cover and
cook at 100% for 15 minutes or until
the potatoes are cooked.
— Add the milk, savory, salt and pepper
and stir.
— Heat at 100% for 4 to 5 minutes before
serving.

Fish and Leek Soup

Ingredients
225 g (8 oz) fish fillets, cut into pieces
175 mL (3/4 cup) leeks, white parts only,
sliced across
50 mL (1/4 cup) olive oil
1 onion, finely chopped
375 mL (1-1/2 cups) clam juice
500 mL (2 cups) white wine
50 mL (1/4 cup) long grain rice
pinch curry powder
salt and pepper to taste

Method
— Pour the oil into a dish and add the
onion and leeks.
— Cook at 100% for 3 minutes, stirring
once during the cooking time.
— Add all the other ingredients and mix
well.
— Cover and cook at 100% for 10 to 13
minutes, stirring three times during the
cooking.
— Season to taste before serving.

MICROTIPS

**What Makes a Really Good
Fish Stock?**

Fish stock, also called
fumet, is certainly the best
stock to use as the base in
many types of fish soups. It
is obtained by poaching fish
in a small amount of water
along with herbs and
aromatic vegetables and is a
wonderful addition to fish
broths and bisques. It can
also be reduced and added
to other soups to give them
a distinctive flavor.

Many of the regions in
which a great deal of
seafood is used in their
cooking have their own
special recipes for fish
stock. However, experts
agree that fish stock made
by simmering the fish
heads, bones and trimmings
along with the ingredients
described above produces an
incomparable fish stock.

Oyster Soup

Ingredients
625 mL (2-1/2 cups) oysters, with their liquid
50 mL (1/4 cup) butter
1.125 L (4-1/2 cups) hot milk
125 mL (1/2 cup) white wine
pinch nutmeg
pinch paprika
salt and pepper to taste
chives to garnish

Method
— Put the oysters and their liquid with the butter in a casserole.
— Cook at 100% for 3 minutes, stirring once during the cooking time.
— Add the hot milk, wine, nutmeg and paprika.
— Reduce the power level to 90% and heat for 4 to 5 minutes, stirring twice during the cooking time; do not allow the soup to boil.
— Season to taste and garnish with chives before serving.

Shrimp Bisque

Ingredients
340 g (12 oz) uncooked shrimps, shelled
500 mL (2 cups) chicken stock
15 mL (1 tablespoon) butter
50 mL (1/4 cup) rice
15 mL (1 tablespoon) onion, grated
175 mL (3/4 cup) white wine
125 mL (1/2 cup) 35% cream
salt and pepper to taste

Method
— Pour 250 mL (1 cup) of the chicken stock into a dish with the butter; add the rice and onion and cook at 100% for 3 minutes; reduce the power level to 70% and continue to cook for 5 minutes or until the rice is done.
— Purée the mixture at high speed in a blender, adding a little of the remaining chicken stock.
— Stir the purée into the last of the stock and set aside.
— Pour the wine into a dish and add the shrimps; cook at 100% for 4 to 5 minutes or until the shrimps are cooked.
— Set a few shrimps aside to use as a garnish and purée the others with the wine in the blender.
— Combine the two blended mixtures; cover and cook at 100% for 4 to 5 minutes or until the soup reaches the boiling point.
— Add the cream, season and mix well.
— Reduce the power level to 70% and heat through for 1 to 2 minutes.
— Garnish with the reserved whole shrimps before serving.

Compound Broths

Compound broths are based on broth, to which a number of different ingredients including rice, noodles, barley, vegetables, meat, poultry or fish may be added in varying combinations. They differ from thick soups in that the ingredients are sliced or diced and not puréed; retaining their shape and their texture, the ingredients can be identified.

As their name suggests, these soups may be composed of ingredients from the same family, such as a variety of vegetables, or ingredients from very different food families, such as a combination of meat, vegetables and rice. In either case, it is customary to include roughly equal quantities of each ingredient.

Compound broths are similar in many ways to stews and often include the same ingredients—the same types of meat, aromatic vegetables and seasonings. The difference lies in the fact that these soups contain fewer solid ingredients in proportion to the amount of liquid than do stews and that their ingredients are usually chopped more finely. For this reason, care should be taken in preparing compound broths because overcooking the chopped ingredients will spoil both their texture and their flavor. A useful tip is to chop all the ingredients roughly the same size so that they cook evenly. Once cooked, each should have its own distinctive flavor and texture, a characteristic that particularly applies to this type of soup.

If you are one to feel that all this precision is just too complicated, there is another approach that is less troublesome and just as efficient. Simply add the ingredients in stages, depending on how long each takes to cook. Begin with those that cook the most slowly and add those that cook more quickly a little later.

If you want a first class compound broth that is based on meat, select a cut of beef, veal or lamb that has a bone. Choose quality meat that will be meltingly tender once it is cooked. The same can be said for such soups based on chicken. It is also important to select other ingredients with flavors and textures complementary to the meat chosen as well as the right combination of aromatics. And don't forget that pasta, rice and barley make hearty additions to these soups.

Enjoy trying different combinations to come up with your own perfect compound broth!

Chicken and Ham Soup

Ingredients
250 mL (1 cup) cooked chicken, cut into strips
250 mL (1 cup) ham, cut into strips
30 mL (2 tablespoons) butter
1 stick celery, finely sliced
1 carrot, diced
1 onion, finely chopped
1.5 L (6 cups) chicken stock
pinch thyme
salt and pepper to taste

Method
— Put the butter in a dish and heat at 100% for 30 seconds; add the celery, carrot and onion.
— Cover and cook at 100% for 4 to 5 minutes, stirring once during the cooking time.
— Add the stock, thyme, ham and chicken.
— Cover and cook at 100% for 10 to 12 minutes, stirring twice during the cooking time.
— Season with salt and pepper and serve.

Ham and Watercress Soup

Ingredients
250 mL (1 cup) ham, cut into fine strips
250 mL (1 cup) watercress, chopped
1.25 L (5 cups) water
5 mL (1 teaspoon) salt
30 mL (2 tablespoons) tomato paste
5 mL (1 teaspoon) tarragon
2 egg yolks
30 mL (2 tablespoons) 35% cream
pepper to taste

Method
— Put the water, salt, tomato paste, tarragon and watercress in a casserole; cover and cook at 100% for 10 to 12 minutes, stirring twice during the cooking time.
— Add the ham, cook at 100% for 4 to 5 minutes and set aside.
— Mix the egg yolks with the cream and then beat with a whisk.
— Slowly add 50 mL (1/4 cup) of the hot cooking liquid to the egg and cream mixture, whisking constantly.
— Combine the egg and cream mixture with the hot liquid, beating all the while.
— Season to taste before serving.

MICROTIPS

Freeze Leftover Rice and Use It in Soup

How many times do you find that you have cooked too much rice? When you do, don't throw it away. You can freeze it and defrost it later in your microwave without losing any of its flavor or nutritional value.

If intended for use in soup, freeze lefover rice in containers that will hold 125 mL (1/2 cup) or 250 mL (1 cup) at most. Seal, date and freeze. Rice will keep in the freezer for up to six months. When you want to defrost it, put the container in the oven and microwave at 70%. A 125 mL (1/2 cup) quantity

of rice takes between 2 and 3 minutes to defrost while 250 mL (1 cup) will take between 4 and 8 minutes. Stir twice during the defrosting process.

In adding defrosted rice to soup, don't add it until the last minute; if you add it earlier it may well overcook.

Chicken Liver and Rice Soup

Ingredients
225 g (8 oz) chicken livers, cut into small pieces
175 mL (3/4 cup) rice
2 L (8 cups) chicken stock
30 mL (2 tablespoons) butter
grated Parmesan cheese to taste
salt and pepper to taste
15 mL (1 tablespoon) parsley, chopped

Method
— Pour the chicken stock into a casserole dish and heat at 100% for 13 to 15 minutes.
— Add the rice, cover the dish and cook at 100% for 15 minutes.
— Put the butter in another dish and heat at 100% for 30 seconds; add the chicken livers and cook at 70% for 4 to 5 minutes, stirring twice during the cooking time.
— Add the cooked livers to the stock and rice.
— Sprinkle with Parmesan, stir and season.
— Garnish with parsley before serving.

Barley and Vegetable Soup

Ingredients
75 mL (1/3 cup) barley
125 mL (1/2 cup) celery, diced
125 mL (1/2 cup) onion, diced
125 mL (1/2 cup) carrot, diced
1 540 mL (19 oz) can tomatoes, chopped
1.5 L (6 cups) beef stock
salt and pepper to taste

Method
— Pour the stock into a dish and bring to the boil by heating at 100% for 13 to 15 minutes.
— Add the barley and vegetables; cover and cook at 100% for 40 to 45 minutes, stirring twice during the cooking time.
— Season to taste and serve.

MICROTIPS

To Cook Asparagus, Broccoli and Cauliflower for Cream Soup

A number of cream soups are based on asparagus, broccoli and cauliflower. These vegetables are cooked and then puréed and the purée is added to stock. The resulting soup is reheated for just a brief period of time to avoid the destruction of any nutrients.

You must take care to arrange asparagus and broccoli spears correctly to cook them in the microwave oven. They should be placed in a large glass dish, their tips pointing toward the center. Add just 125 mL (1/2 cup) water and cover with plastic wrap.

To cook cauliflower cut it into flowerets of equal size, arrange them in a round glass dish and add 50 mL (1/4 cup) water. Cover with plastic wrap.

As for power levels and cooking times, follow the instructions in your recipe, keeping the quantity being cooked in mind. It is important not to overcook the vegetables, but they must be soft enough to purée.

Tomato and Noodle Soup

Ingredients
1 540 mL (19 oz) can tomatoes, chopped
125 mL (1/2 cup) small noodles for soup
1.25 L (5 cups) water
savory to taste
2 shins of beef
4 carrots, diced
2 sticks celery, diced
1 540 mL (19 oz) can tomato juice
salt and pepper to taste
parsley, chopped

Method
— Pour the water into a casserole and add the savory and shins of beef; cook at 100% for 30 to 40 minutes, stirring once, and skim the surface.
— Add the carrots, celery and tomatoes and continue to cook at 100% for 15 to 20 minutes or until the vegetables are done.
— Remove the beef shins and add the tomato juice.
— Cook at 100% for 3 to 4 minutes and then add the noodles.
— Cook at 100% for another 4 to 5 minutes, stirring once during the cooking time.
— Season to taste and sprinkle with parsley before serving.

Vegetable Soup

Ingredients
250 mL (1 cup) cabbage, cut into strips
125 mL (1/2 cup) carrot, diced
125 mL (1/2 cup) rutabaga, diced
125 mL (1/2 cup) celery, diced
1 onion, finely sliced
50 mL (1/4 cup) butter
1.25 L (5 cups) hot beef stock
salt and pepper to taste
10 mL (2 teaspoons) fresh parsley, chopped

Method
— Put the butter in a casserole and heat at 100% for 40 seconds; add all the vegetables, cover and cook at 100% for 5 to 7 minutes.
— Add the hot beef stock and season.
— Cook at 100% for 13 to 15 minutes or until the vegetables are done.
— Check the seasoning and adjust if necessary; add the fresh parsley before serving.

MICROTIPS

Homemade Soups in a Hurry

When you're short of time, you probably don't even consider making soup because you have grown up thinking that it must be simmered for hours. However, if you have leftover cooked meat or poultry on hand, you can make your own soup very quickly in the microwave oven. For example, with just 250 mL (1 cup) of cooked chicken, you can make a highly nourishing homemade soup for four people in less than 20 minutes. All you do is combine the chicken with 625 mL (2-1/2 cups) hot water, 175 mL (3/4 cup) egg noodles, 125 mL (1/2 cup) frozen vegetables, 15 mL (1 tablespoon) chicken powder concentrate and the appropriate seasonings. Then cook the soup no longer than 15 minutes at 100%.

This basic recipe can be varied to suit the ingredients you have on hand. They may include cooked beef, pork or lamb (which should be cut into small cubes) and cooked vegetables, legumes, rice and so on. Dare to experiment and you will likely come up with some winning combinations of your own.

Chicken Noodle Soup

Ingredients
1 chicken carcass
250 mL (1 cup) egg noodles
1.5 L (6 cups) water
15 mL (1 tablespoon) poultry seasoning
125 mL (1/2 cup) celery, finely sliced
30 mL (2 tablespoons) mixed herbs
pepper to taste
parsley, chopped

Method
— Pour the water into a casserole, add the chicken carcass and the poultry seasoning; cook at 100% for 60 minutes, remembering to turn the carcass over halfway through the cooking time.
— Remove the carcass and strain the stock through a fine mesh.
— Add the celery and herbs to the strained stock and cook at 100% for 10 minutes.
— Add the egg noodles and continue to cook at 100% for 4 to 5 minutes or until the noodles are done, stirring once during the cooking time.
— Add the pepper and sprinkle with parsley before serving.

Chicken and Rice Soup

Ingredients
250 mL (1 cup) chicken, cooked and diced
125 mL (1/2 cup) rice, cooked
1 small onion, chopped
1 L (4 cups) chicken stock
salt and pepper to taste
parsley, chopped

Method
— Put the onion in a casserole and cook at
  100% for 2 minutes; add the chicken
  stock and continue to cook at 100% for
  4 to 5 minutes.
— Add the rice and the cooked chicken
  and cook at 100% for 6 to 8 minutes.
— Season and sprinkle with parsley before
  serving.

MICROTIPS

To Clean Mushrooms

Fresh mushrooms usually have a little of
the soil in which they were grown clinging
to them and most people simply wash it
off under running water. This method,
however, is really not the best. Mushrooms
are very porous and absorb the water
easily, which can result in cooked
mushrooms that are rather tasteless. Is
there a better way? Yes—simply brush
them clean with a special soft brush.

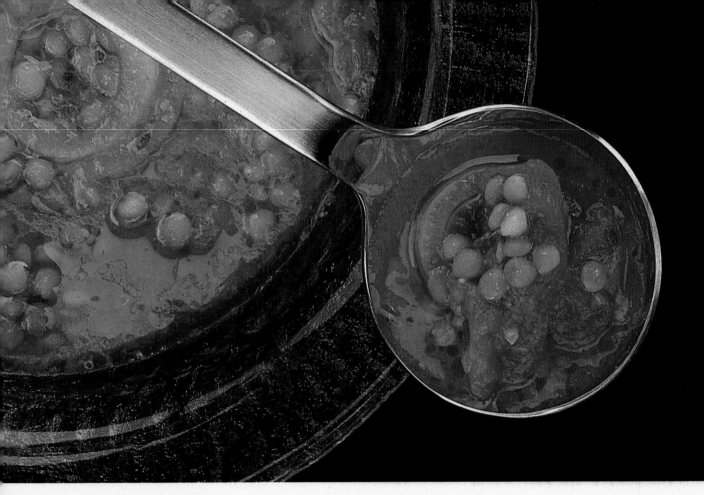

Lentil Soup

Ingredients
250 mL (1 cup) lentils
1 L (4 cups) boiling water
1 796 mL (28 oz) can tomatoes, chopped
1 large onion, finely sliced
15 mL (1 tablespoon) dill seed
2 cloves garlic, crushed
2 bay leaves
salt and pepper to taste

Method
— Pour the boiling water into a casserole and add the lentils; cook at 100% for 10 minutes.
— Allow to stand for 30 minutes.
— Add all the remaining ingredients; cover and cook at 100% for 15 minutes.
— Stir, cover again and cook at 100% for 1 to 1-1/2 hours, stirring twice during the cooking time.
— Check the seasoning and adjust if necessary; remove the bay leaves before serving.

Cabbage Soup

Ingredients

1 L (4 cups) cabbage, chopped
45 mL (3 tablespoons) butter
2 onions, chopped
375 mL (1-1/2 cups) leeks, white parts
only, sliced across
5 mL (1 teaspoon) salt
2 mL (1/2 teaspoon) pepper
2 mL (1/2 teaspoon) sugar
1 L (4 cups) beef consommé
250 mL (1 cup) hot milk
250 mL (1 cup) carrots, grated

Method

— Put the butter in a casserole and heat at
  100% for 40 seconds; add the cabbage,
  onions, leeks, salt, pepper and sugar.
— Cook at 100% for 4 to 6 minutes; add
  the consommé and cook at 100% for 15
  minutes.
— Blend in the hot milk; check the
  seasoning and adjust if necessary.
— Add the grated carrots and cook at
  100% for 3 to 4 minutes before serving.

Onion Soup au Gratin

Ingredients

2 large onions, sliced into fine rounds
1 L (4 cups) boiling water
2 beef stock cubes
50 mL (1/4 cup) butter
salt and pepper to taste
4 slices crusty bread, toasted
250 mL (1 cup) Swiss cheese, grated
paprika

Method

— Pour the boiling water into a bowl, add
  the beef stock cubes and set aside.
— Put the butter in a dish and heat at
  100% for 1 minute; add the onions and
  cook at 100% for 5 to 6 minutes;
  season and add the prepared beef stock.
— Put the soup into 4 individual bowls
  and lay a slice of bread on top of each.
— Sprinkle each slice of bread with grated
  cheese and paprika.
— Reduce the power level to 90% and heat
  through for 8 to 10 minutes.

MICROTIPS

To Wash Spinach

Spinach can be such a nuisance to
wash that one could be forgiven for
resigning oneself to the idea that
crunching on a little grit is the price
that must be paid for enjoying its
distinctive flavor. However, there is an
easy way to wash spinach so that it is
really clean. Put the leaves in a large
bowl of cold water and swish them
around gently with your hands. The
gritty sand will sink to the bottom. Lift
the spinach out and put it into a
collander to drain.

Minestrone Soup

Ingredients
75 mL (1/3 cup) navy beans
115 g (4 oz) bacon, diced
1 clove garlic
1 onion, finely sliced
2 potatoes, diced
2 carrots, sliced
2 sticks celery, sliced
1 tomato, peeled and chopped
15 mL (1 tablespoon) tomato paste
2 L (8 cups) beef stock
1/2 small cabbage, grated
250 mL (1 cup) frozen peas
1 zucchini, cut in half lengthwise and finely sliced
125 mL (1/2 cup) butterfly-shaped pasta for soup
2 stalks parsley
grated Parmesan cheese to taste

Method
— Put the beans in cold water in a covered bowl and leave to soak for 8 to 12 hours.
— Leave the cover on and cook at 100% for 11 to 13 minutes or until the beans are done but still firm, stirring once during the cooking time; drain and set aside.
— Put the bacon in a casserole and cook at 100% for 3 to 4 minutes.
— Add the garlic and onion; cover and cook at 100% for 3 to 4 minutes, stirring once during the cooking time.
— Add the cooked beans, potatoes, carrots, celery, tomato, tomato paste, 500 mL (2 cups) of the beef stock, cabbage, frozen peas and zucchini; cover and cook at 100% for 17 to 19 minutes or until the vegetables are *al dente,* stirring twice during the cooking time.
— Add the remaining beef stock and bring to the boil by heating at 100% for 13 to 15 minutes, stirring once during the cooking time.
— Add the pasta and parsley; cover and continue to cook at 100% for 4 to 5 minutes, stirring once during the cooking time.
— Sprinkle with the Parmesan and serve hot.

Pea Soup

Ingredients
450 g (1 lb) yellow peas
225 g (8 oz) salt bacon, diced
3 L (12 cups) water
3 onions, finely sliced
2 carrots, diced
2 bay leaves
5 mL (1 teaspoon) savory
salt and pepper to taste

Method
— Put all the ingredients together in a casserole.
— Cover and cook at 100% for 25 to 30 minutes or until the mixture reaches the boiling point, stirring once during the cooking time.
— Allow to stand for 1 hour without removing the cover.
— With the cover still on, cook at 100% for 60 minutes or until the peas are cooked, stirring several times.
— Remove the bay leaves and adjust the seasonings. This soup can be served as it is or puréed in a blender.

Home-Style Soup

How did grandmother make that wonderful soup that you remember so well? Was the secret in the choice of ingredients or in the way she cooked it? The truth of the matter is that our grandmothers rarely followed any specific recipe; they used their experience and their own judgment to make the best of whatever was available and added aromatics and seasonings until it was just right.

Ingredients
30 mL (2 tablespoons) butter
1 onion, chopped
1 clove garlic, finely chopped
1 540 mL (19 oz) can tomatoes
2 stalks parsley
salt and pepper to tate
1 L (4 cups) chicken stock
125 mL (1/2 cup) alphabet noodles

Method
— Put the butter in a casserole and heat at 100% for 30 seconds; add the onion and garlic and cook at 100% for 1 minute.
— Stir in the tomatoes, parsley, salt and pepper and cook at 100% for 2 to 3 minutes.
— Crush the tomatoes with a spoon and add the stock.
— Cook at 100% for 8 to 10 minutes and add the noodles.
— Continue to cook at 100% for 4 to 5 minutes, stirring halfway through the cooking time.

Cold Soups

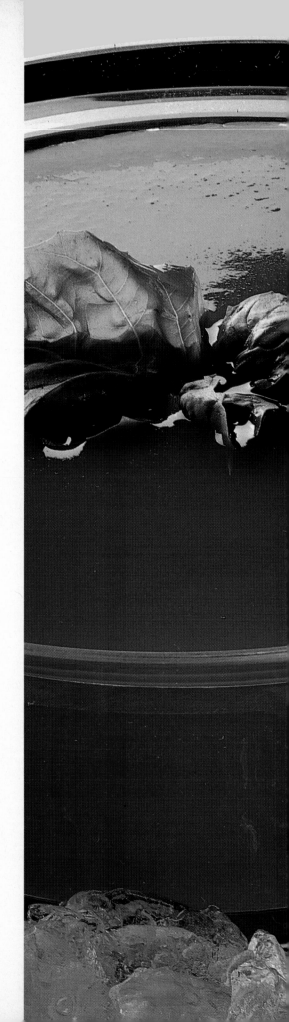

Here comes summer, and it's time to revamp not only your wardrobe but your menus as well. Why not try a cold soup? In a country such as Canada, where the winters are so long, cold soup may strike many as quite a novelty if not a real oddity. However, it is really worth a try. Some cold soups are made with uncooked ingredients while others are cooked and then chilled. They are light, nutritious and healthy and make wonderful, vitamin-packed additions to any well-balanced diet.

Cold soups provide a great opportunity for you to show off your cooking skills. In selecting the right ingredients, the most pleasing combinations of flavor, texture and color may be obtained—stimulating the eye as well as the palate.

Gazpacho, one of the cold soups most familiar to us, is Spanish in origin. Consisting of a tomato base with finely chopped vegetables from the typical Spanish kitchen garden, it is an extremely refreshing summer soup.

With the help of a blender or food mill, you can turn all kinds of fresh vegetables into delicious cold soups. For maximum flavor, however, you should not always chop the ingredients too finely as some cold soups are better for having a certain amount of texture.

Summer is also the season when fruit is available in abundance, and it should not be overlooked as a possible ingredients for cold soups. Fruit alone or fruit in combination with vegetables make lovely summer soups. Surprised? Perhaps you are, but it is worth experimenting. Pears, for instance, go well with watercress and apples with carrots.

In the following pages we provide you with a few ideas for cold soups. And don't forget that many of our recipes for hot soups are equally good served cold. You simply cook them and chill them in the refrigerator. It may be necessary to alter one or two details, but the basic approach is the same. A classic example is Cream of Leek, which can be served cold as Vichyssoise, either as a starter or as a meal in itself.

Many bisques are also excellent when served cold.

However, it is important to remember that chilled food loses some of its flavor, so the seasoning should be checked before serving a cold soup.

Unfortunately, we don't have the space to deal with the endless list of soups that can be served cold, so we would encourage you to experiment with a number of them to find out for yourself which ones are your favorites!

Pear and Watercress Soup

Ingredients
8 pears, very ripe
2 bunches watercress, leaves and stems, chopped
1 L (4 cups) chicken stock
125 mL (1/2 cup) 35% cream
30 mL (2 tablespoons) lemon juice
salt and pepper to taste

Method
— Peel and core the pears, reserving the cores and peeling.
— Put half the chicken stock in a bowl; cut the pears into quarters, immersing them in the stock to prevent them from discoloring. Set aside.
— Put the remaining stock in another bowl and add the cores and peelings; cover and cook at 100% for 8 to 10 minutes to extract maximum flavor and then strain.
— Add the watercress to the strained broth; cover and cook at 100% for 8 to 10 minutes.
— Add the pear quarters and their stock to the hot broth and purée in a blender.
— Add the cream and lemon juice and season to taste.
— Refrigerate for a few hours before serving.

Gazpacho Soup

Ingredients
125 mL (1/2 cup) chives, finely chopped
250 mL (1 cup) parsley, finely chopped
125 mL (1/2 cup) chervil, finely chopped
1 clove garlic, crushed
1 green pepper, diced
2 large tomatoes, peeled, seeded and chopped
125 mL (1/2 cup) olive oil
50 mL (1/4 cup) fresh lemon juice
1 Spanish onion, finely sliced
1 cucumber, diced
salt and pepper to taste
3 slices bread
500 to 750 mL (2 to 3 cups) light stock or tomato juice, as desired

Method
— Put the chives, parsley, chervil and garlic in a bowl with a little of the oil and pound vigorously to make a paste.
— Add the green pepper and tomatoes.
— Add the olive oil slowly, stirring constantly.
— Add the lemon juice, onion and cucumber; season with salt and pepper and set aside.
— Heat the slices of bread at 100% for 3 to 4 minutes to dry them; crush the white part and add to the mixture or set aside to use as a garnish.
— Add the desired quantity of liquid and chill for 3 to 4 hours in the refrigerator; check the seasoning and adjust if necessary.
— Put in individual serving bowls and add an ice cube to each.

MICROTIPS

Coconut: The Secret of Really Great Chilled Soup

If you like to experiment with different flavors, creating chilled soups is a great way to show off your skills. When you make soups that are to be served hot, you must be careful not to add too much in the way of seasonings. But because the flavor of cold food is usually more bland, you can be more generous with the seasoning and experiment a little.

One flavor that is quite intriguing and very original is that of coconut. Try adding a little coconut milk just before you serve the soup. Then grate a little of the coconut itself to garnish each serving or allow your guests to help themselves. A little startling, perhaps, but different!

Vichyssoise

Ingredients
30 mL (2 tablespoons) butter
2 leeks, white parts only, finely sliced
1 small onion, finely sliced
1 potato, finely sliced
625 mL (2-1/2 cups) hot chicken stock
salt and pepper to taste
125 mL (1/2 cup) 35% cream
45 mL (3 tablespoons) chives, chopped

Method
— Put the butter in a dish and heat at 100% for 30 seconds; add the leeks, onion and potato and cook at 100% for 5 to 6 minutes.
— Add the hot chicken stock, salt and pepper; stir and cook at 100% for 14 to 16 minutes.
— Sieve the mixture and chill for several hours.
— Add the cream and mix well just prior to serving. Garnish with chives.

MICROTIPS

Vichyssoise

Vichyssoise is a cold soup based on the classic recipe for cream of leek and potato soup, which is traditionally served hot. The vichyssoise that we know today was invented in the United States by a French chef, but the term itself now sometimes pertains to soups that are really variations, based on different ingredients but prepared and served in the same way. These soups are frequently referred to as being "servi en vichyssoise."

Good vichyssoise differs from hot cream of leek and potato soup in two ways; less butter, optional in the hot soup but which would solidify in a chilled soup and ruin its consistency, is used in vichyssoise and a larger quantity of fresh cream is added. Note that it is best to add the cream to the chilled soup just prior to serving because the basic purée thickens to quite an extent in the chilling process. You are then able to add the cream in the quantity needed to achieve the consistency you want.

Sauce and Soup Terminology

Over the course of its history cooking, like all great arts, has developed its own specialized terminology. The terms may refer to characteristics of the dishes themselves or to techniques employed in their preparation. As you will encounter many of them frequently in this volume, we thought it would be useful to define some of the more common ones.

Clear Soup: A light soup make with meat, poultry or fish stock that has been reduced to some extent to make a broth. It may be clear or it may contain a few other ingredients, such as finely diced vegetables and/or meat.

Compound Broth: Soup made with broth as its base but differing from clear soup in that it contains a large number of ingredients, such as meat, poultry or fish; diced vegetables; and pasta, rice or barley, in varying combinations. The addition of the quantity of ingredients makes it a more hearty soup than clear soup.

Consommé: Meaning "consummate broth," consommé is made with meat, poultry or fish stock that has been concentrated to an extent greater than that for a light broth. A successful consommé is extremely flavorful and perfectly clear.

Cream Soup: A thick, puréed soup to which cream is added to give it a smooth consistency.

Deglaze: To add liquid such as water, stock, a good dry wine, cream or vinegar to a dish in which meat, poultry or fish has been cooked in order to make use of the flavorful juices that have seeped out during the course of the cooking.

Fond: The French term for a concentrated stock used as a basic ingredient in sauces and soups.

Fumet: A strongly flavored fish stock made by boiling the heads, bones and any trimmings of fish; used as a basic ingredient in many sauces for fish and fish soups.

Garnish: A garnish is to food what an accessory is to clothing, an added decorative touch that makes it more appealing to the eye.

Poach: To lightly simmer meat, poultry or fish in a liquid, such as water or stock, with aromatic herbs and vegetables.

Puréed soup:	A soup made by cooking ingredients, usually vegetables, in stock and then sieving or blending them until they are smooth and creamy.
Reduce:	To boil a mixture to evaporate surplus liquid, thereby concentrating the flavor and producing a thicker consistency.
Roux:	A mixture of flour and butter in equal quantities that is cooked until the desired color is obtained and used as a thickening agent in many sauces.
Scald:	To bring a liquid almost, but not quite, to the boiling point. Milk, for example, is frequently scalded before being added to roux to make béchamel sauce.
Season:	To add salt, pepper, herbs and spices to food in order to enhance its flavor.
Simmer:	To cook over a gentle heat without allowing the mixture to come to a full boil.
Skim:	To remove fat (or impurities) from the surface of a stock or a sauce. One simple method is to chill the mixture, allowing the fat to form a solid layer on the top, and then simply lift it away.
Stock:	A flavored liquid obtained by boiling a large quantity of water with the bones and trimmings of poultry, meat or fish and a combination of aromatic herbs and vegetables. Used as a basic ingredient in many sauces and soups.
Thicken:	A procedure in which a heavier consistency is given to liquid that is too thin. A number of thickening agents can be used to thicken soups and sauces. Examples include puréed starchy vegetables, roux, a mixture of cold water and flour or cornstarch and, for a really smooth consistency, cream and egg yolks.

Culinary Terms

Have you ever been faced with a menu and found yourself unable to understand some of the terms used to describe the dishes on it? Of the many culinary terms that exist, the majority are French in origin. To help you find your way about, here is a short list of terms and their meanings.

Aioli: A cold sauce made with mayonnaise as its base and heavily laced with garlic; it goes especially well with potatoes, meat and salads.

Béchamel: A white sauce made with cream or milk in which roux is used as a thickening agent. It is flavored with onions, salt, pepper, nutmeg and/or bay leaves, depending on the recipe used.

Créole: A spicy sauce made with tomatoes, garlic, onion and crushed peppers mixed with a little white wine and seasoned with cayenne.

Danoise: A thick sauce made with a mixture of chicken stock, puréed mushrooms, cream and fine herbs.

Gasconne: A velouté sauce made with veal stock and fine herbs cooked in white wine and blended with anchovy butter.

Madrilène: Chicken consommé with concentrated tomato pulp and seasoned with cayenne. Served very cold.

Maria: Soup made with beans, carrots and rutabagas to which cream and chervil are added. A traditional soup in Quebec.

Provençale: A sauce made with tomatoes and garlic as main ingredients to which parsley, pepper, a pinch of sugar and white wine are added.

Scotch broth: A traditional soup made with tender chunks of lamb, diced vegetables and barley.

Suzette: A velouté soup made with mushrooms and watercress and garnished with fine strips of green beans.

Conversion Chart

Conversion Chart for the Main Measures Used in Cooking

Volume
1 teaspoon............ 5 mL
1 tablespoon........ 15 mL

1 quart (4 cups)....... 1 litre
1 pint (2 cups)....... 500 mL
1/2 cup........... 125 mL
1/4 cup........... 50 mL

Weight
2.2 lb.......... 1 kg (1000 g)
1.1 lb................ 500 g
0.5 lb................ 225 g
0.25 lb.............. 115 g

1 oz.................. 30 g

Metric Equivalents for Cooking Temperatures

49°C.............	120°F	120°C.............	250°F
54°C.............	130°F	135°C.............	275°F
60°C.............	140°F	150°C.............	300°F
66°C.............	150°F	160°C.............	325°F
71°C.............	160°F	180°C.............	350°F
77°C.............	170°F	190°C.............	375°F
82°C.............	180°F	200°C.............	400°F
93°C.............	200°F	220°C.............	425°F
107°C.............	225°F	230°C.............	450°F

Readers will note that, in the recipes, we give 250 mL as the equivalent for 1 cup and 450 g as the equivalent for 1 lb and that fractions of these measurements are even less mathematically accurate. The reason for this is that mathematically accurate conversions are just not practical in cooking. Your kitchen scales are simply not accurate enough to weigh 454 g—the true equivalent of 1 lb—and it would be a waste of time to try. The conversions given in this series, therefore, necessarily represent approximate equivalents, but they will still give excellent results in the kitchen. No problems should be encountered if you adhere to either metric or imperial measurements throughout a recipe.

Index